Praise for *Five St*

'The book takes the mystery aw; normalises our reactions, thereby to feeling afraid or panicked or d(this book to anyone who wants to learn how to develop skills to handle the challenges of life.'

Niamh Fitzpatrick, Psychologist Olympic Council of Ireland.
Agony Aunt Ray D'Arcy Show Today fm.

'The language is simple and the author gives clear examples of how real individuals perceive and make sense of their difficulties rather than catastrophizing each event. This book will benefit both therapists and patients in putting their knowledge of CBT into action.'

Joanne Fenton, Consultant Perinatal Psychiatrist, Coombe Women and
Infants University Hospital

'Enda has a unique gift with trainees and clients. I've been lucky to have Enda as a mentor and trainer in CBT . . . So learn from the best. Read this book.'

Lisa Fitzpatrick. Stylist and TV presenter

'Written in concise, understandable, plain language [this book] will prove to be an invaluable reference for both people and GPs alike.'

Dr Owen Clarke, Director, North East specialist GP training scheme.

'Accessible, easy to read, practical . . . This book which the author defines as "not another self help book" leads us gently to uncover habits of unhappiness and discover how instead to "learn to be the fool occasionally" . . . What freedom! Enjoy the journey!'

Dr Miriam Kennedy, Consultant Psychiatrist, St Patrick's hospital

'Enda Murphy says it all when he states "Be very careful who you let into your mind" . . . This book challenges the reader to question their thoughts and make the changes that are needed for a better quality of life . . . an outstanding read.'

Maria Carmody, President of NCPII / Director of Corporate Affairs for
the Irish College of Humanities & Applied Sciences

First published in 2013 by
Liberties Press
140 Terenure Road North | Terenure | Dublin 6W
Tel: +353 (1) 405 5703
www.libertiespress.com | info@libertiespress.com

Trade enquiries to Gill & Macmillan Distribution
Hume Avenue | Park West | Dublin 12
T: +353 (1) 500 9534 | F: +353 (1) 500 9595 | E: sales@gillmacmillan.ie

Distributed in the United States by
Dufour Editions | PO Box 7 | Chester Springs | Pennsylvania | 19425

Distributed in the UK by
Turnaround Publisher Services
Unit 3 | Olympia Trading Estate | Coburg Road | London N22 6TZ
T: +44 (0) 20 8829 3000 | E: orders@turnaround-uk.com

ISBN: 978-1-907593-86-4
2 4 6 8 10 9 7 5 3 1
A CIP record for this title is available from the British Library.

Cover design by Ros Murphy
Internal design by Liberties Press

Five Steps to Happiness

Learning to Explore and
Understand Your Emotional Mind

Enda Murphy

A note on the text

This book is primarily written for people who suffer from panic attacks, anxiety and depression.

In this book we will meet numerous people who have come to see me for help over the years. Ordinary people like you and me who found themselves in an emotional hole that they couldn't figure how to get out of.

However, I would hope that it will also prove essential reading to:

- Anybody interested in why these conditions occur
- Families and loved ones of sufferers
- Therapists and health professionals who have an interest into how Cognitive Behavioural Therapy works in real life.

I have identified five habits people commonly engage in that cause unhappiness. Learning to avoid these will form the basis of the five steps to happiness. Once you start reading the book, you will probably want to jump straight into the five habits immediately and if you do then feel free to do so.

However you will also find chapters on other mental health issues like why we feel what we do and how we go from mental health to mental ill-health.

Understanding the explanation of the habits is fairly straightforward. Explaining the explanation is the difficult part. Hence the other chapters on mental health.

This is because very few people understand how emotions are caused and where they come from. And unless we understand why it is we feel what we do, then we can't understand why sometimes it all goes wrong for us.

Translating complex theory into a format that people can readily understand can be extremely difficult. I have found that an easy way to do this is to illustrate the theory by telling the story of someone who has experienced the particular problem.

If you read their stories, I hope that you will be able to identify with them and more importantly understand how they and you can solve the problem.

So without any further ado, let's meet the cast!

Contents

Foreword

Dr Harry Barry

I am delighted to have been asked to write a foreword for this wonderful book. I met Enda back in 2004 and it was from the beginning a meeting of minds. We both share a passion for simplifying and normalising the whole area of mental health. Enda is not only an excellent CBT therapist in his own right but has spent the past seven years in particular teaching family doctors through the ICGP and GP training schemes a completely new approach to the management of common mental health difficulties.

At the heart of Enda's philosophy is a deep caring for those in mental distress and a kindness and empathy which comes through in every page of this excellent book. He is the creator of the Raggy Doll concept, which many of those who have read my own books will be familiar with. This simple but profound concept is but one of many wise and practical pieces of advice he has for those in trouble.

But this book is meant for each and every one of us. For all of us as human beings fall into the five unhealthy habits so wonderfully presented in it. Do we not all spend our lives, for example, rating ourselves or living in a world where our happiness depends on our perceptions of how others view us? Do we also not spend so much time trying to control life? In particular do we not spend so much of our lives abnormalising the normal? Such habits have a great capacity to make us feel unhappy and unfulfilled in life.

There will also be many who pick up this book who may have battled against panic attacks, general and social anxiety, depression and eating disorders and whose lives are often wasted by not receiving help in time (before these conditions become chronic). There are many books out there packed with information about these conditions but that do not really show us how to solve them. This is what is so special about this particular book – for it *focuses on the solution and not just the problem*!

I have spent the last few years trying to persuade Enda to write this book, for I like many of my colleagues have learnt so much from him. His approach has always been hands-on and totally practical – based more on emotional intelligence. I feel his wisdom and solution based approach to the emotional problems many of us face in our lives will assist us in dealing with such issues.

Enda and I both believe that we need to present mental health in a completely new manner with particular emphasis on lifestyle and reshaping many of the thinking and behavioural habits behind common mental health difficulties. There are many families throughout our country who are grieving over the deaths of loved ones to suicide. There is little doubt in my mind that the concepts in this book go a long way to addressing many of the reasons for the emotional distress that drive so many down this dark road and offers solutions as to how to deal with them.

My congratulations to Enda (and his lovely wife Mei who has been such an inspiration in his life) for the wonderful work he is doing and for producing this excellent book which has so much potential to change the lives of many.

Dr Harry Barry
(GP and author)

Chapter 1

Not Another Self-Help Book

Louise's Story

Louise sat in the coffee shop and despaired once again about the future. No matter how hard she tried she just couldn't work out how other mothers coped with their children, or more importantly, why she couldn't. The harder she tried, the worse she seemed to be doing.

She looked down at her sleeping baby in the pram. Thank God he was asleep. As she looked at him she reflected, as she often did these days, that the only peace she got now was when he was asleep. Not that she could call this peace. It was just another form of misery, her head whirling around and around, getting herself worked up into a state about how much she was failing at this 'motherhood'.

Sometimes she thought that she must be a complete failure. Surely if this was what she was biologically designed to do, then why sweet God could she not just be as good as the other mums in her area, who she saw each day with their kids, wheeling their prams, and generally just doing what normal mums did?

And that feeling of being a complete and utter failure was getting worse and worse. What other conclusion could she come to? All the other mothers were doing fine. Since she was doing so badly, there must be something wrong with her. She glanced across the café at the woman with blonde hair who was sitting there. Louise was used to seeing her around the area but never had the courage to say hello as she was afraid that if she did, the woman would see how bad a mother Louise was, and hate her almost as much as Louise hated herself.

How difficult should this be? Alright, she knew that it would be difficult; everyone said that it would be. But they all seemed to be just getting on with it, whilst here she was, walking miles and miles every day pushing the pram as it was the only way she knew to keep the baby quiet. And that was as good as it got, just managing to keep him quiet.

As she looked at the blonde woman feeding her baby she felt the tears starting to fill up behind her eyes. 'Oh God, look at how in control she is, and look at me.' Louise got up quickly and rushed to pay her bill. The blonde woman smiled at her as she passed by, but Louise just brushed past with barely a glance, her whole focus was on getting away before she burst into tears and showed the whole world what a dreadful mother and a person she was.

As she reached the path outside the café her mind started to settle a little. Out here on her own with the baby she felt a little safer. At least whilst she was walking, she only had to deal with her own sense of failure, without the whole world having to see it.

She found walking eased the head a bit, gave her time to think. But the thoughts, whilst they always started out as positive, trying to figure out a solution and resolving to try harder in the future, invariably turned back into nightmares, until she was once again flogging and loathing herself at how poorly she was doing.

'How did my mother cope? She had four of us. And I never saw her cry once. Sure she used to get frustrated from time to time, what mother wouldn't? But no matter how bad she got she was always able to cope. Not like me, I panic at the slightest thing. I have a husband who is caring and supportive, live in a nice house and have no money worries, not like poor Michelle across the road. Her husband has just lost his job and look at her, she's still able to cope.'

'Not like me. Nothing to worry about but I'm still panicking. Oh God I must be the most selfish bitch in history and what about my husband. I know he is really missing the intimacy we used to share.'

'He can be so sweet and supportive. He would never put any pressure on me to have sex, but I just know he's feeling the pressure too and that makes me feel even worse. How could I be so selfish? I can't even think about sex without breaking out into a cold sweat.'

Suddenly her baby started to waken and cry, looking to be fed. Oh Jesus thought Louise, please don't start crying. I can't cope with this. With a rising sense of panic she looked into her bag for his bottle.

Damn, she thought, I should have got the café to warm it up before I left. That's what a proper mother would have done.

Quickening her stride, she headed back to the café. Oh please stop crying, she pleaded silently to her baby. Oh God, what if your woman is still there when I go back in, she thought. Oh god, please have left by the time I get back.

Living in Your Head

Sound familiar? Well, this is what it's like to be living inside your own head when you're struggling with feeling down. In Louise's case, her 'down' feelings were being triggered by having to look after a baby.

But you don't have to have children to feel like this. Perhaps you don't have children at all, but have you ever felt that everyone else is normal except you, that no matter what you do, no matter how hard you try, you can't figure out what's wrong with you?

You feel as if, when you were being made your head was accidentally wired by . . . the plumber. Why can other people figure all this out so easily but you can't? What do they have that you don't?

Well, that is why I've written this book – to try to help you understand why you are feeling the way you are and more importantly what you can do about it.

Or as I was taught in college, the *real* skill in being a therapist is not only to give the client the tools to develop good mental health, but to show the person how to use them.

When it was first suggested to me to write a self-help book based on my experience as a Cognitive Behavioural Therapist, I declined as I thought that the last thing this world needs is another self-help book. And even if I did write one, what would make it different to many of the excellent ones out there?

After talking at length with numerous clients, friends and colleagues, what did become very clear was that self-help books don't work for a lot of people. Indeed, for lots of people, they don't need *another* self-help book. Being able to put into practice what all the other ones say would be enough.

You see, for lots of people, the problem isn't that they need another way of doing it. For them, understanding why *they* can't do what other people take for granted is the real issue.

From talking to clients and colleagues, it became clear to me over time that what was needed was a book that would go some way towards taking the mystery out of mental health.

Understanding Our Minds

Our understanding of how our minds work is being

improved every day. In theory, understanding what makes us tick should make it easier to practise healthy mental habits in real life.

In practice however, it isn't easy at all. Translating theories into practical solutions is a lot harder than you think. There is a saying that the person who invented the wheel was an idiot, the *real* genius was the person who invented the other three.

And this is very true. The more I thought about it the more I realised that what was needed was a book that could translate complex psychodynamics into a simple framework that people could easily understand. To explain what mental health is, how we get it, how we lose it and most importantly how to get it back when we've lost it.

It was when I spoke to a client called George though that I realised that there were more equally valid reasons why a book like this was sorely needed. What do I mean? We'll try this. Define *mental health* for me. What is it?

Take some time to think about your answer. Surely something that most people take for granted should be easy to define. And as you've guessed by now, it isn't that easy to define, is it?

Therefore, this book will go some way towards explaining precisely what mental health is and dispelling some of the absolutely ludicrous myths about mental health that I see being sold as fact. Furthermore, this book will use plain language to explain what it's all about. Of course the *true* goal is to try to put all this into a framework that people can understand easily.

As George explained, 'Nobody had ever explained to me why I was feeling the way I was. I never knew why other people could do it but I couldn't. Everybody could tell me what I needed to do. In fact I knew myself what I should be doing. The problem was that nobody was able to teach me how to do it. I didn't need support, I needed a solution. It was like knowing that I needed to get to Galway, but neither knowing how to read a map nor how to drive a car. I could see everybody else doing it but hadn't a clue how to do it myself.'

Teaching you the 'what, why and how' of mental health is only *one* reason for writing this book however. From talking to people, another need that people have is to gain *hope* that there is a solution out there for them, understanding that you are not helpless like a piece of driftwood floating on an emotional sea, powerless against the current. That even though you may feel that you cannot change the circumstances around you, you *can* change the way you feel about them.

But before we go any further, let's meet some more people who we are going to come back to throughout this book who you might identify with.

Hilda's Story

Hilda stood in the queue in the local post office. She hated having to do it. Thursdays were always the worst. Ever since she had started having the panic attacks she would avoid crowded places like this like the plague. It was only because she *had* to queue to get her social welfare that she was here. The queue seemed to be taking an age to move. 'Oh God', she thought, 'please don't let me have a panic attack here.'

Just then she noticed her legs beginning to shake. She felt her breathing become more rapid and a kind of shakiness occurring in her chest. Oh no, she realised. It's starting again.

The shakiness started to get worse and worse and with it she could feel her heartbeat getting faster and faster. She felt that her heart was beating so hard that it was going to burst out of her chest. The shaky feeling started to spread to the rest of her body. She could feel the pins and needles in her arms and legs. Her throat felt like it was tightening and with it she started feeling that she couldn't catch her breath.

She started to look frantically for the door. All she could see were the people between her and the door. There was no way of getting out fast without pushing people out of her way. Oh Jesus, she pleaded. What am I going to do now? Everybody's going to see me.

Laura's Story

Laura put the phone back in its cradle. Why had she done that? Why had she agreed to go to Terry's leaving party? She dreaded the thought of the whole evening. Everybody would be there and she just couldn't face meeting them all at one time, walking into the room and everybody looking at her.

This party would be like every other party. Laura would try to make conversation but, as would happen at every other one, she just wouldn't know what to say. People would make polite conversation for a few minutes and then would find an excuse to walk away. She could just imagine them laughing and chatting with their friends.

Why couldn't she be like them? All Laura was able to do was blush if someone spoke to her, showing everybody how much of a loser she was.

'And that's exactly what I am, one big loser. All people have to do is look at me and they can see what I'm really like. Other people have so much confidence. People like them. Not like me,' she thought. 'Even in school the bullies used pick me out of the others in the class. Why can't I just get people to like me?'

For Laura, facing each day was so hard; thinking that she was one of life's big rejects. All she wanted to do was to sit down and cry. She had read all the self-help books but they all made it sound so easy. 'All I have to do is change, but change what? It seems so easy for other people.

Laura's sister kept suggesting going to a self-help group but the thought of sitting in a group with all the other 'losers' in life just made her want to cringe. 'I hate myself,' she said to herself for the thousandth time. 'And now I have to go to this bloody party and let everyone see me for what I really am.'

Kathy's Story

Kathy woke up in the early hours of the morning as she frequently did these days. The anxiety was there as usual like a cold dread in the pit of her stomach that no matter what she did, she just couldn't shake. Martin, her husband, was still asleep.

'In the past I used be able to call him when I felt like this,' she thought. 'But not now. Now even he is getting frustrated that I won't accept what the doctors keep telling me.'

It had all started one day while she was looking in the mirror. Laura had noticed that a freckle on her face looked slightly different. She wasn't too worried about it but as she had lost her own mother from cancer two years previously she thought she had better get it checked out, just to be on the safe side. Of course with all the things she had to do that day it would just have to wait.

Her day was more focused on trying to get the contract agreed. Her company could really do with it, and she, as usual being the golden girl, was trusted to get it through. '*Me*', she thought, 'I've always been able to deliver. That's why I'm the director of sales isn't it?' This time though, the goalposts were different. What with the credit crunch and all that. She just wasn't as confident as she usually was.

It was as she was taking off her make-up that night,

getting ready for bed that she noticed the freckle again. Surely it wasn't the same as when she looked at it this morning. She found herself staring at it for a long time and twice during the night she woke up thinking about it. She went into the bathroom each time and examined it minutely. The more she looked at it the more alarmed she got.

Next morning she rang the office to say she'd be in late and went immediately to her GP's surgery to see him. Her GP listened carefully to her story and then carefully examined the freckle. He reassured her that it was normal and was the same as the few other freckles that she had. This reassured Kathy and she headed off into work. She had enough to worry about regarding this bloody contract without having to worry about bloody freckles, she laughed nervously.

During the day however she just couldn't focus on her work. The more she tried the more she thought about what the GP had said. 'How could he be so sure?' she thought. 'He doesn't know my freckles that well. How would he know it hasn't changed, it definitely looks different to me. Perhaps I should get some tests or at least get a referral to a specialist.'

And that was the start of the nightmare. She had pestered the GP into referring her but the specialist told her the same thing. His reassurance only reassured her for a few days. Then she started to doubt even his word. If this wasn't enough she then started to worry that maybe there might be something else wrong with her. Things got worse and worse. She lost the contract and her boss was on her back.

Her period was a bit heavier than usual that month but no matter how much she or her GP tried to convince her she didn't have cancer she still couldn't let it go and kept worrying about it. Now she found that no amount of reassurance from her GP worked. She worried about every little thing and she just had to be checked out by a specialist for everything.

Martin had been very supportive at the start, reassuring her and all that. But now even *he* was getting exasperated just like the rest of her family when she tried to talk about it. 'Can you not just see that there's nothing wrong with you?' they would say when they became frustrated. Now she tried not to talk about it at all. What was the point? Talking only made it worse.

And that was the infuriating thing about this. At one level she could see she was being illogical, but regardless of the efforts she made she couldn't shake the anxiety and accept that there was nothing wrong with her. Her work had suffered so much that she dreaded going into the office in the mornings. She even dreaded getting new assignments now. How could this have happened to her? She had always been so confident and self-assured. Wasn't she always the one people turned to for advice when things went wrong?

'Now look at me. A complete nervous wreck'

Ordinary People

What do all these people have in common? You might think not a lot, but as we will find during the course of this book, they have more in common with each other than you would think. For starters they were all feeling miserable and they had no idea why they were feeling like this or more importantly what they could do to make the problem go away. They represent a reasonable cross section of people who look to me or indeed any other mental health professional for help.

They're ordinary people, no different from you and me, who found themselves with a problem that they couldn't fix themselves, but were able to learn how to fix it for themselves when they were given the tools to do so.

Three other things they have in common is that they

finally decided enough was enough and sought help. The person these four people approached was their GP (who was a member of the CBT project run by the Irish College of General Practitioners) and through their GP, they ended up at my door. Most importantly, however, they are all now living happy, contented lives, free from the torture that had become their existence.

As we go through this book, we will be meeting Louise, Hilda, Laura and Kathy again along with lots of other people who have come to see me over the years. We will look at what was really causing the problem, and how you and I do the same things and make the same mistakes as they do.

The cases are real, too. Everybody mentioned has given permission for me to use their story to show that mental health and happiness is not rocket science when you have a way of simplifying it and understanding why it is we feel what we do.

One of the reasons self-help books can be difficult to implement in our lives is that they try to translate theory into a pragmatic method of self-help. This is notoriously difficult to do in mental health as the psychodynamics of mental health (psychobabble to you and me) can be very complex. It's a bit like expecting to be able to experience the flavour of a particular dish when all you have to go on is the list of the ingredients.

In this book I use authentic stories because I have found that most of us find it much easier to learn when we can identify with something or somebody. And once you experience the flavour of what mental health is all about then achieving it isn't all that complicated.

I have found that over the years, when we run into a mental health problem we all have a tendency to make very similar mistakes and that most mental health problems are the result of people making one or more of five basic errors.

These five basic errors are the reasons that many people find achieving good mental health so difficult. I've called these errors the Five Habits.

A large proportion of my work as a Cognitive Behavioural Therapist is in teaching people how to correct these errors in thinking. I emphasise the phrase 'teaching people *how* to correct' as I believe that in the world we live in today people are looking for solutions and any form of psychotherapy that fails to provide workable solutions for people are in serious danger of losing their relevancy.

That is why the emphasis in Cognitive Behavioural Therapy over the last few years has been to discover and provide brief, practical interventions that can be used in everyday life. We have been very lucky in this country. The need for this type of 'low intensity' CBT approach was identified by the Irish College of General Practitioners way back in 2001 and a training programme was established to teach GPs practical CBT interventions which could be used to help people to overcome the most frequent mental health difficulties.

A similar programme was set up by Merchants Quay Ireland for addiction councillors and health professionals for use in their clinical practices when a CBT approach was needed. A specific model of CBT was established for use in these programmes and to date over 750 GPs and health professionals have completed the programme, making it the oldest and at one time the largest programme of its kind in the world.

Facilitating Change

Ideology is the luxury of those who don't have to live with or sort out the mess. Having worked at the coalface of mental health for over thirty years, I, like a lot of my colleagues do not have the luxury of living with theory. When someone approaches us for help, those of us who work at the delivery end are faced with the unenviable task of trying to find some way whereby theory can be made workable. This means identifying interventions that work and discarding ones that don't.

The skills and insights I try to give in this book are based on my experience in the field of mental health. Some of them are mine but the vast majority are skills and insights I have learned from some of the most wonderful people I have met on my journey through life.

All I have done is to put them into a framework which I believe will make mental health easier to understand and which can be applied to specific problems in our lives, and more importantly make it easier to find and implement solutions.

Chapter 2

Habit 1: The Panic Attack Cycle

So let's start with the first habit. In describing the habit though, I'm going to do it in a slightly different way. As I said in the first chapter, the purpose here is not to give you a list of mental health 'ingredients' and hope that you will be able to make a cake out of them yourself; the purpose is to try to give you 'emotional insight' into understanding why the problem is occurring and what the habit is all about.

Emotional insight is where we understand/see something at an emotional level. It is where our logical and emotional minds are in agreement with each other.

As we will see later on, when we have both logical and intellectual insight at the same time, we are in our 'wise mind'. Sometimes this is just called 'insight'. But regardless of what title you give it, the meaning is still the same.

Gaining emotional insight is one of the primary goals in CBT. It is an essential part of the therapy process. It is where we translate theory into practice. An example of where you experience emotional insight regularly is when you are trying to understand something and 'the penny drops'. This 'penny dropping' is your logical and emotional minds synchronising with each other, giving you a new understanding of the issue.

When teaching, I try to give trainees this kind of insight into the difficulties that they see people having. How I do this is to illustrate the theory by showing it in a case history. I'm going to do the same here.

By recounting a case history and explaining the theory of *why*, I hope that you will understand both at a logical and emotional level, why the person, and perhaps yourself are experiencing what you are.

Hilda's Story

Hilda (who we last met in Chapter 1) arrived at my clinic on a very wet and windy morning. I can remember her arrival well as when she first sat down she commented in her fine County Louth brogue that she wasn't sure which was worse, the weather or her mood.

She outlined what had happened in the post office that day. She related that after she got home from the post office she decided that enough was enough and finally plucked up the courage to ring me.

I asked her what was different about this particular panic attack, as opposed to every other one, that made her lift the phone this time. Hilda wasn't quite sure why this time was different, nor did she understand the relevancy of the question.

I explained that by asking, and getting her to think about the answer, we were starting a process whereby Hilda, instead of just accepting what was happening to her, would start questioning herself more and more as to why her problem was occurring and why she was sitting with me.

You see, all behaviour has purpose. We don't just do things willy nilly. Most of the time we aren't even aware as to why we behave the way we do, but that doesn't mean there isn't a reason.

Cognitive Behavioural Therapists are like detectives. We are always looking for the reason why someone is sitting with us. However learning to recognise why you act and think in certain ways is a lot harder than you think.

Most of us either don't think about it too much or spend our time convincing ourselves of the logic and justification for why we're acting in a certain way i.e. believing our own bullshit.

Alcoholics Anonymous has a slogan taken fom *Hamlet*: 'to thine own self be true.' Contrary to what a lot of people think, this does not involve being totally honest with the world, rather it has to do with being honest with yourself.

Members learn that to remain sober they must always be aware of the real motives behind their actions. This is very true for the rest of us too. As humans we all have a huge ability to convince ourselves of anything.

So that was why I asked Hilda what on the surface might seem a fairly innocuous question, but in reality can open up a whole new world of understanding.

The End of the Road

Hilda said that as she left the post office she felt as if her whole world had just crumbled around her. She had been fighting these panic attacks for the last five years and regardless of what she did, she was powerless over them.

They had not only totally taken over her life, but when she wasn't having them, she lived in constant dread of one occurring. As she left the post office she felt as if she had no more fight in her. They had won.

She felt as if the gates of hell were opening and she couldn't stop herself falling through them. She walked home in a state of total despair. It was only as she arrived home that she remembered the phone number that her GP had given her during one of her many visits over the years about the same problem.

Hilda felt that she had nowhere else to turn. Her family were supportive but they were as helpless as she was. She had very little faith in what I could do, but as the saying goes, 'you'll never find an atheist in a soldiers foxhole', so she decided she had nothing to lose and to give it a go.

Seeking Help

There is an old joke that asks: *How many psychotherapists does it take to change a light bulb?* The answer is: *One, but the light bulb has got to want to be changed.* This was true of Hilda.

And there's nothing wrong with that. When we run into emotional trouble, most of us try to rely on our own resources first. That's all well and good, but we all have a tendency to keep relying on our own resources even when they are blatantly not working.

Of course, if you eventually conclude that your own resources are not working, what do you do then? Well the healthy thing to do is to tell someone. Sometimes by just hearing yourself speaking, solutions can become apparent.

However, if after you have spoken to someone the problem is still there, then what? Well when this happens, you need professional help or a 'professional ear'. Because that is precisely what a therapist is: a professional ear. Someone who is trained to *actively listen* to you. By doing this they can then help you untangle what's going on in your head.

So this is where Hilda and I started, trying to figure out why it was this time that she reached out for help. After a wee bit of discussion about what was different this time, Hilda concluded that, yes, what was different about this time was that she was sick and tired of being . . . sick and tired.

Even though she didn't realise it at the time, at a subconscious level she had thrown in the towel. She had unconsciously concluded that she couldn't resolve this on her own and was going to have to rely on someone professional to help her confront the issue.

Furthermore, what she realised was that this time she was willing to stop trying to do it her way and start learning another way. This was a very important conclusion for Hilda to arrive at because it freed her to start making the necessary changes.

The Panic Attack

Now we were ready for the next step. You see, being *willing* to change is only the first step. You could describe it as 'the push' to the starting gate. However the starting gate is just that, the start. We still had to solve the problem.

Having ascertained that Hilda was ready to start learning a new way of dealing with her panic attacks, we went on to the next stage of the therapy, finding out why the problem was occurring. So to help us, I asked Hilda to describe her last panic attack.

Once again this is harder than you might expect. Quite often when I ask people this question, they try to give me *their* interpretation of what happened to them. Using terms like 'It was as if' when they try to describe what they think was happening to them.

It can be very frustrating for the person when I interrupt them by gently challenging them about what they mean by certain metaphors and similes. More than once I've been accused of not listening.

What the person doesn't realise is that not only am I listening, but that I am listening *intently* to what they are saying. It's actually they who are are not listening to themselves. What they are doing is accepting at face value what their emotional mind is telling them.

This is usually vague and unclear, but when people are

experiencing panic attacks their conclusion is usually very definite, i.e. 'I'm going to die' or something like that.

Hilda described standing in the queue at the post office and said she suddenly started to feel very shaky. She felt her breathing become more and more rapid, and a kind of shakiness occurring in her chest.

This shakiness started to get worse and worse and with it she could feel her heartbeat getting faster and faster. She felt that her heart was beating so hard that it was going to burst out of her chest. She felt her legs tremble with pins and needles and thought she was going to collapse.

Her head was pounding and she could feel herself shake all over. Hilda felt that she needed to get out of there fast, that if she didn't get out then something dreadful was going to happen to her.

When I asked her what she thought *was* going to happen, she said she wasn't sure but it wasn't going to be good. All she could remember at the time was that the sensation was getting worse and worse, and looking frantically for the door.

The queue was so backed up that she felt that she was not going to make it out to the street. That was when she felt the panic take over completely. She could feel herself sobbing with fear. Hilda described the feeling of terror as she inched her way to the door.

It was with a huge sense of relief that Hilda eventually made it outside. All she could remember was seeing the sunlight. As she made her way down the street, she felt the symptoms starting to abate. She made her way back to her car, and it was only when she was safely inside that she felt the flood gates open.

Hilda started to cry as she recounted how she felt as if the gates of hell had opened up in front of her. There was nothing she could do. She was desperate. She would eventually succumb totally and 'go mad or something like that'.

Going Back to the Beginning

Having gotten to the end of the story I asked Hilda to go back to the start so we could look again at what happened. I asked her that as the panic was taking hold and during the episode, what precisely was she afraid was happening to her?

Hilda by this time was getting used to me asking searching questions like this, and that's probably why she didn't just finish me off on the spot for not listening properly the first time.

'What do you mean?' she retorted. Did I not understand what she had just told me? She had this feeling of impending doom which, she believed, would engulf her if she didn't get out of the post office.

'But, what would have happened if you hadn't been able to get out? Let's say for example I had super-glued your feet to the floor so that you couldn't have escaped. What would have happened then?' I asked.

Hilda was lost, she wasn't quite sure what would happen if she didn't get out of there, but she sure as hell wasn't staying to find out. 'And have you ever stayed to find out?' I asked. Hilda said no, and that in all honesty she didn't know what would happen. All she knew was she had to get out.

We then looked at some more examples of where she had had panic attacks. And do you know what? In all the examples Hilda gave, a certain pattern began to emerge. One was that she felt something dreadful was going to happen, and two, that she ran before she could discover what, in reality, would happen.

Understandable when you look at it. Most of us would react in the same way. However by always running when the panic occurred, Hilda had convinced herself that something dreadful would happen if she stayed.

Instinctive Reaction

You see, having a reaction like Hilda's is perfectly normal. Believe it or not, if we didn't have this type of reaction we would have never evolved from being monkeys. Something would have eaten us all up a long time ago.

When something happens to us we process what is happening in two parts of our brain, namely our logical and emotional minds. Did you ever find yourself in two minds about something? Well this is your emotional and logical minds in conference with each other.

We will be looking more closely at how these two minds interact with each other in Chapter 5, but for now let's look at what was happening in both Hilda's emotional and logical minds at the time of her panic attack.

To do this let's look first at what the primary purpose of our emotional mind is. Believe it or not the main purpose of our emotional mind is to *protect* us first and foremost. And how it does this is truly amazing.

Try to think of your emotional mind as a form of radar. It is constantly scanning your environment looking for danger. It does this by continuously looking at what is happening in your environment, scanning things looking for any potential danger.

If your emotional mind does see a potential danger, it doesn't hang about. Like a smoke censor in a fire alarm, once it detects smoke it doesn't wait to see if there is a fire or not. It just sounds the alarm. As any fire fighter will tell you, when you hear a fire alarm, you *get out*. Only when you are out do you look back to see if there was a fire or not.

Our emotional mind works in kind of the same way. When it sees a potential danger it immediately sends a signal to our adrenal glands. We have two of these, one sitting on top of each kidney.

Fight or Flight

On receiving the danger signal, our adrenal glands go into action by producing adrenaline. It does this so fast and the resulting reaction is so rapid, our logical mind can't keep up.

By producing adrenaline, our emotional mind and adrenal glands trigger what we call the Fight or Flight response. The adrenaline that is released by your adrenal glands causes changes in your body which will enable it to either fight its way out of danger or run like the wind to get away (flight).

This adrenal reaction is automatic and is vital for our survival. If you can imagine you're a caveman and have suddenly been confronted by a saber-toothed tiger that wants to eat you, then you don't have the luxury of sitting around deciding what the best course of action is. The adrenaline fight or flight response makes you respond instinctively to bring you somewhere safe.

We can describe this by comparing your emotional mind to a jet aircraft suddenly launching down the runway. Your logical mind is you running after it. When the aircraft reaches the end of the runway, instead of taking off, it stops dead with its engines screaming! This is because, having got you to react and got you to a place of relative safety, it now holds you at that point.

Your logical brain meanwhile has been plodding along behind. By plodding along much more slowly it is able to look carefully to see whether the danger is real or not. It takes some time to catch up with your emotional 'jet', but it eventually does if you let it.

If your logical brain spots some real danger then it will help you decide on what further action is required, e.g. keep running. However if your logical brain decides that the danger is not real and that it wasn't a saber-toothed tiger but a domestic cat, it sends a message to your adrenal glands to switch off the fight or flight response.

34

Looking More Carefully

So let's apply this theory to Hilda's panic attack. What was happening with Hilda was that her emotional brain was doing exactly what it is supposed to do. It was sensing a potential danger and reacting exactly as it was supposed to.

Hilda, however, wasn't allowing her logical mind to catch up. Or at least if she was, she couldn't hear or recognise what it was saying. Unfortunately for her, instead of ascertaining whether there was a real danger or not, Hilda, by consistently running and not looking back, was reinforcing the belief that something dangerous was happening.

Over time, by always running, the tiger's teeth in her mind were getting bigger and bigger. By never looking back, or to be more to the point, by not knowing how to look back, she couldn't see what she was running from, or whether it was something she needed to run from or not.

Even though she was convinced that something bad would happen to her, she couldn't pinpoint what. Poor Hilda just kept running every time it happened and didn't know how to stop running. By the time Hilda reached me she had lost all ability to be able to think or act rationally when her emotional fire alarm went off.

After I explained this, Hilda thought about it for a while. She eventually volunteered that she had never looked at it this way. 'You see, I have always just run out of where I was,' she said. She had always just accepted what she believed was happening to her.

Gently, I explained that now she needed to stop blindly accepting her thinking and start questioning it. I then suggested that we go back a bit so I could start showing her how to do this. I explained to Hilda that what causes us to feel what we do is not determined by what happens to us but by how we interpret it.

Armed with this new piece of information I again asked

Hilda to think about the incident and what was going through her mind at the time. As she spoke, I wrote her answers on a whiteboard in my room.

Hilda thought for a while before confiding what was going through her mind at the time. She thought her heart was going to burst and that if she didn't do something to prevent it, she would have a heart attack.

Cognitive Pathways

So now let's look at Hilda's panic attack in a clear light and look at what was going on in her head at the time. When something happens to us we all follow a thinking pattern in our minds. We call this a 'cognitive pathway' which can be simplified like this:

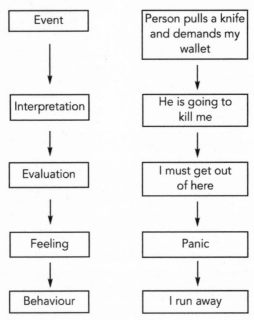

Fig. 1: Cognitive Pathway

Understand? Well now, let's simplify this chain reaction even more, so that it makes more sense in everyday language. To do this I'm going to change the terms slightly. In place of the word 'event', I'm going to use the word 'trigger'.

This is because the event is actually a trigger for the chain reaction that results in what we feel. In Hilda's case, the trigger was all the physical symptoms she was feeling.

Sometimes, though, identifying the trigger can be more difficult for people. Usually this is because many people who have panic attacks are looking for the trigger in the wrong place. Alas, this can send you off on a wild goose chase looking for clues in all the wrong places.

Common Mistakes

The mistakes I most commonly find people making are that they look for some reason or clue in the actual environments where the panic attacks are actually taking place.

For example, people will go to great lengths to describe where and when the panic occurs. Instead of looking at what is happening to them at the time, they look at what in the environment may be triggering it. They may describe how it happens in one supermarket, but are baffled as to why it doesn't happen in another.

Or they may say that it happens when they are with people they don't know and not when they are with people they do know. Or maybe even vice versa. Either way, looking for some cause in the environment is of no use. The environment is not causing the panic attack. All the environment is doing is triggering a chain reaction.

It's quite irrelevant where it happens. What is relevant is what is happening at the time, and the common denominator between all the circumstances in which you experience the panic is the fact that it is the same chain reaction that is happening each time.

We've all heard the expression 'I couldn't see the wood for the trees'. This expression is very apt when it comes to panic attacks. We can only see the trees (the environment) but can't see the wood.

In the case of panic attacks, the wood conveys the physical symptoms that you are experiencing and *it is your interpretation of these physical symptoms that causes the problem*. Not the symptoms themselves.

Realising this can be very empowering. You see, by grasping that it's your interpretation of the symptoms you're experiencing and not the symptoms themselves that are causing the problem, it is much easier to fix. Why should this be empowering? Because it means it is not necessary to stop the panicky feeling happening, in order to be able to stop the panic attack.

And as we shall see, trying to stop the panicky feeling happening is about the worst thing you can do. Ignatius Loyola, who founded the Jesuit Order, said 'What you resist will persist.' And this is no truer than in panic attacks.

Confused? Well if you only learn that when you start feeling panicky, it is what you say to yourself about what is happening that causes the panic, then that's enough for now. So let's elaborate our understanding further, and go back to Hilda.

Finding the Danger

In Hilda's case, having identified a specific trigger from a specific incident, we were ready to start looking at what she was saying to herself about it, i.e. her interpretation.

In trying to provide simple clarity to what's going on, I'm going to replace the word 'interpretation' with the word 'danger'. The reason for this is that when we feel anxious, our interpretation is always in the form of attaching some form of danger to the trigger.

When panic attacks occur, the danger we attach to the trigger is always one or more of four primary dangers. We say to ourselves that because we are experiencing the symptoms, we are going to:

> 1. *Die*: That the symptoms are so dangerous that I'm going to have a heart attack, stop breathing or some other potentially lethal result.
> 2. *Go Mad*: That things will get so bad that I will lose my sanity.
> 3. *Do Something*: I will lose control of my behaviour and run amok around the room/airplane etc.
> 4. *Be Derided*: People will see me, and what will they think.

In Hilda's case, she was afraid she was going to die. When she looked at the dangers, Hilda revealed that she had also believed that if she didn't get out, the symptoms would drive her mad.

Either way, we now had two pieces of the puzzle. The first was that she had various physical symptoms; the second that she would either die from a heart attack or would go mad if she didn't 'escape'. So let's put these two pieces of the puzzle into our formula:

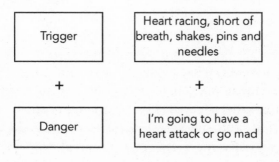

OK so far? Well if you are, then you have now taken a major step in identifying what was going on in Hilda's head, and possibly your own, when panic attacks occur. Now let's go a bit further.

You see, finding the trigger and danger is only part of what we have to do to find the solution to Hilda's panic attacks. In order to understand why they were occurring we need to look further at Hilda's reaction to her interpretation that she would go mad or die. That is, her behavioural reaction – how she responded and why.

Hilda, when she panicked, would automatically run away. We call this running away 'safety behaviour'. In CBT terms, safety behaviour is behaviour we use to attempt to protect ourselves.

Unfortunately as we shall see, our attempt to protect ourselves has the opposite result. In Hilda's case as with all people who are experiencing panic attacks, safety behaviour has the effect of actually increasing the amount of danger they think they are in.

The Final Piece

Having got Hilda to identify her safety behaviour, i.e. running away, the next step was to help her understand what she was trying to achieve by running away. In order to protect herself, what was Hilda trying to get rid of?

Finding this final piece is essential if we are to understand exactly why Hilda's panic attacks were happening. Look at her safety behaviour again. By running away, Hilda was trying to satisfy a demand that, 'in order to protect myself, I must get rid of the physical symptoms that are dangerous. Otherwise I will die or go mad.'

Now let's put Hilda's experience into this formula.

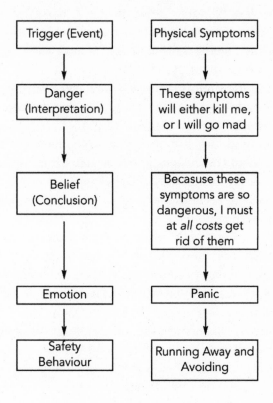

Fig. 2: Cognitive Pathway

We now have all the pieces of the puzzle. But that is all we have, the pieces of the puzzle. This is the hard part; you see, unless you know how to look at these pieces, you will never see the obvious reason as to why Hilda was having panic attacks.

Thinking Like a Therapist

Now comes the technical bit. If you want to understand why panic attacks occur and how to get rid of them, then you have to learn how to think like a therapist.

To do this I have to take a little time out to introduce some basic CBT therapist skills that are essential if you are to understand the rest of this chapter.

Looking at the information that we have so far, you would be forgiven for thinking that maybe figuring this out should be easy. Not so.

Most of us go through life never asking ourselves why we come to certain conclusions about certain things. In fact lots of people never need to. It's only when we run into trouble that we need to backtrack and look at what we're saying to ourselves more closely.

The reason is that when something happens to us, we don't consciously think up our interpretations/evaluations. They happen at the speed of light. Remember, when we have a thought, a message must be transferred from one part of the brain to another.

In order to do this the thought must be converted into an electrical signal. And electricity travels at the speed of light. What this means for us is that our interpretations and conclusions often occur so fast that we aren't even aware of the pathway.

So why do these electrical signals take different pathways in people? Why, when something happens, do some people interpret it in one way, and some people another?

Our cognitive pathways are developed as a result of what we call our *nature versus nurture*. Nature refers to your genetic makeup; and nurture to what you have learned from your experiences.

A close friend and colleague, Dr Harry Barry, in his book *Flagging the Therapy*, does a wonderful job of explaining the neuroscience behind our emotions, or to put it simply he explains the *electrics* of why we feel what we feel without the jargon.

You don't have to look too far though to see this science in real life. We all react differently to different situations. Look around you and notice how people react in lots of different ways to similar situations. It's what makes us all different.

However, when we get into difficulties with anxiety and depression we have a tendency to make the same 'thinking' connections in our emotional heads that cause the problem.

In the case of panic attacks, the person is attaching a danger to what is physically happening to them. Now this may seem fairly straightforward to you. It's not, however, for it's only by understanding where attaching danger to the physical symptoms gets you, will you understand why panic attacks occur.

Simple But Not Easy

Now that we have all the information necessary to understand Hilda's panic attacks, let's put them all together and solve the problem. If you look at the trigger you will see that in all the circumstances where Hilda got panicky you will see that what they all had in common is that they all trigger an adrenaline reaction.

Let's look at this adrenaline reaction in more detail. Remember, as I've already said, the adrenaline reaction is our bodies' way of triggering our fight or flight reaction.

How it does this is once adrenaline is secreted into our blood stream by our adrenal glands, the adrenaline has an instantaneous and very powerful effect on our body. Adrenaline acts on our body by:

> 1. Dilating the blood vessels in our arms, legs and head. This is so as much oxygen carrying blood can be pumped into your arms so you can fight your way out of danger (the more oxygen, the more strength), your legs so you can run your

way out of trouble and your head so you can think and react faster.

You will notice this reaction by the symptoms you feel in your body. You may feel:
- your arms and legs getting very shaky
- weakness in your limbs
- maybe pins and needles
- A headache

2. By getting your heart to pump faster, your heart is ensuring that it gets as much blood as possible to where it's needed, i.e. your arms, legs and head. Your heart does this by increasing what we call your *stroke volume.*

Normally your heart pumps out about 280mls of blood each time it beats. By increasing the pressure of each beat, your heart increases the amount of blood pumped into your body.

The consequence of this is that you may feel your heart starting to pound. You may feel that your heart is pounding so hard you feel as if it's going to burst out of your chest (which of course it won't).

3. Because your body is demanding so much oxygen, your lungs now go into overdrive in order to keep up with the demand. You start breathing more rapidly and may feel that you're not getting enough air. You are, but because your body is demanding more and more, you *feel* like you're not.

We call this an 'air hunger'. That is, you *feel* like you're hungry for air. However you're not going short of air. You just *feel* this way. The 'air hunger' is your body's way of telling you it needs as much air as possible to deal with the threat, and making you take in as much oxygen as possible.

4. Because the adrenaline has diverted so much blood into the parts of the body it needs to help you 'fight or flight', it has to take more blood from somewhere.

It does this by closing down the parts of the body that it doesn't need, such as your digestive system. How it does this is by constricting the blood vessels in your stomach and intestines.

The consequence of this is that because your stomach is constricted, you may feel nauseous and may even retch. You may also find you get diarrhoea or may even find yourself urinating very frequently. It kind of makes sense that your body does this. The last thing you need when faced with a danger is a full stomach or bladder.

That is what was happening to Hilda when she was in the post office. Her body was doing exactly what it was supposed to do. Her body was reacting to a perceived danger.

However, what was causing the panic attack was not in the environment. The perceived threat was the adrenaline reaction her body was having. The symptoms that she felt were going to kill her were actually those symptoms of the adrenaline reaction that her body was using to try and protect her.

Panicky Feeling vs. Panic Attack

The classical difference between someone getting panicky and someone having a panic attack is that in a panicky situation, the person can identify the trigger. In a panic attack the person can't.

This is because the person doesn't realise that what they are reacting to are the actual physical symptoms of the panic attack. Furthermore, if you believe that the symptoms themselves are going to kill you, drive you mad, run amok or that people will see you, then you will instinctively try to protect yourself by demanding that you must not get anxious.

Trying to satisfy the demand that you must not get anxious is like demanding that you must not think of pink elephants. The more you demand you must not think of pink elephants, the more you will think of them. *The more you demand that you must not get anxious, the more anxious you will become.*

So let's put all the information into our formula:

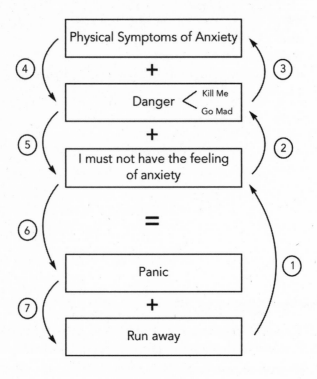

Fig. 3: Cognitive Pathway

Hilda was quite simply getting anxious about being anxious. For Hilda, getting anxious was no longer just an emotion. Hilda believed that the actual symptoms of anxiety were going to kill her.

Dynamics of a Panic Attack

So what would have happened to Hilda if, as I had visualised for her, her feet were glued to the floor in the post office and she couldn't get out?

In Hilda's mind what would have happened, if she hadn't run, was that the symptoms would have kept getting worse and worse so that she would have eventually exploded or 'something like that'.

This is a very common misconception that people have about panic attacks. The belief is that if they were to put the panic attack on a graph (see Fig. 4, line A), the symptoms will keep getting worse and worse.

Most people believe that not only will they keep getting worse and worse, but they will keep getting worse until their heart explodes, they go mad, run amok or whatever other unfortunate thing they think is going to happen.

Hilda, like anyone else, who suffers from panic attacks, didn't realise that this just does not happen. If it did, then adrenaline would not be doing what it's supposed to do. Adrenaline has one purpose and one purpose only, and that is to protect you from danger. One should imagine it as a tool, expertly designed to do this.

If the adrenaline reaction itself was capable of killing you, then you wouldn't need the saber-toothed tiger to do the job, would you? As soon as he started chasing us, we would obligingly pop our clogs for him, saving him the trouble of having to catch us.

And where would that have left the human race but as a readymade snack for any animal that fancied us as an hors d'oeuvres?

Protecting You

Remember, the adrenaline reaction is triggered by your emotional brain. However no matter how panicky you get your logical brain will only let it have 'its head', so to speak, to a certain degree.

This means that no matter how panicky you feel, your logical head will not let you do anything dangerous to yourself.

So now, let's look at what would have happened if Hilda had stayed where she was in the post office and had had her feet glued to the floor.

Keep the images of the jet aircraft racing down the runway in your mind! When the panic reaction starts, your body reacts as I've already described.

However this reaction is self-limiting. That is, the adrenaline reaction, when it starts, can only get to a certain level before it starts to plateau.

If you look at line B in the graph in Fig. 4, you will see this. The panic/adrenaline reaction reaches a certain point, it then stays at that level. This is the jet aircraft reaching the end of the runway and then stopping, but with its engines roaring.

Now imagine yourself running down the runway after the jet. As you are running slower than the jet aircraft, you are able to look more closely around you. In doing so you are able to examine whether the perceived danger that has started the adrenaline reaction is a real danger or not.

As you run down the runway, if you see a real danger then you send a message back to your emotional brain to keep the engines running and take off. But if your brain doesn't find a danger, it sends a message to the emotional brain to switch off the adrenaline engines.

The theory says that the time gap between when the panic peaks and when your logical brain switches it off is twenty-five minutes. In my experience however, I find that this takes about six to ten minutes.

And that is exactly what's supposed to happen. However, in Hilda's case, this wasn't what was happening. As Hilda told me, in her case the feelings were just going on and on . . . and on and on . . . And this had been happening for years.

If my theory is so simple then why was it not working for her? Fair comment, you might say. If the theory was so straightforward then why were her panic attacks continually being triggered?

Making the Problem Worse

Let's look at why this theory wasn't happening in Hilda's case. To begin, let's look at what Hilda was doing that was exacerbating the problem.

For starters, Hilda didn't realise that she was getting anxious about the actual physical symptoms of anxiety. Now this might sound a rather simplistic answer. However if you could only realise the enormous consequence of this error to people's mental health, then you'd understand why so many people suffer so much with panic attacks.

The net result of making this error was that for Hilda, in not realising that it was the actual symptoms of anxiety itself she was attaching danger to, she couldn't for the life of her figure out what the trigger was.

And because she couldn't figure out what the trigger was, her logical brain couldn't switch the adrenaline reaction off. Why would it? If you heard what you thought was a tiger's roar then you'd keep running regardless of whether you could see the tiger or not, wouldn't you?

This is why panic attacks are so debilitating. When they occur, the person can only sense a danger and they then do what any sane person would do . . . They run, or at least they *try* to run.

By the time they have reached my door they have run out of places to run and the panic is catching up with them despite what they might try to do.

Let's look at why this is and what was making Hilda's panic attacks repeat over and over again. If you look at line C on the graph in Fig. 4, you will see that Hilda kept running when she sensed the danger.

By doing so, she was not letting the anxiety/adrenaline reaction reach its plateau. By not reaching its plateau, her logical brain could not switch off the emotional reaction.

It was as if her emotional jet aircraft was still at the end of the runway with its engines screaming at full belt, and Hilda's logical mind, instead of walking to the jet and looking for the danger along the way, had turned tail and ran back to the terminal building instead, leaving the jet engine screaming away at the end of the runway.

Furthermore, when Hilda heard the jet engine screaming, her logical mind concluded that the jet aircraft was coming after her. Therefore she kept running on and on and on. The consequence of this was that the panic, instead of lasting six minutes or thereabouts, was lasting hours, if not days or in some cases weeks (line C).

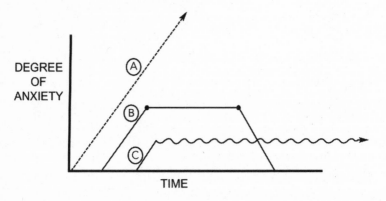

Fig. 4

The Vicious Cycle

Got the idea? Well if you think that's bad, wait until you see what also happens. Look at Fig. 3 and follow the arrows.

Start by looking at Hilda's *safety behaviour*. That is, where she runs out of the post office. Now by running out of the post office she is in a way temporarily satisfying her demand that I *must get rid of the anxiety* (arrow 1).

The result of this is that by satisfying, even temporarily, this demand, she reinforces it in her mind. Imagine that whenever one of your children demanded sweets, you headed off to the shops and bought them sweets. What do you think would happen to their demand for sweets over time?

As any parent will tell you, giving in to your children's demands all the time has the effect of *increasing* the intensity of the demand. This makes them demand more. It also means that the child doesn't learn how to deal with the distress of not having their demand satisfied.

The same goes for us as adults. If we continually demand that we must get what we want then we also inadvertently exacerbate how bad it is when we *don't* get it. This was the case with Hilda's demand. By demanding that she must get rid of the anxiety, she was feeding the problem. The more she demanded that she must not get anxious, the more she was exacerbating how much danger she was really in (arrow 2).

By demanding that she must not have the symptoms, Hilda was inadvertently increasing in her head the danger she would experience if she didn't get rid of them. That is, she was growing the danger of 'I will die, go mad, lose control of my behaviour' etc.

Over time the level of danger she thought she was under, was getting worse and worse. Of course, the result of this was that the more danger she thought she was under, the more and more sensitive to the symptoms of anxiety she was becoming (arrow 3).

As time went on it was taking less and less of these symptoms of anxiety to trigger the danger (arrow 4), which in turn was triggering the demand I must get rid of the anxiety (arrow 5).The net result for Hilda was that she was getting more and more anxious over fewer and fewer physical symptoms of anxiety.

Understanding at an Emotional Level

Essentially, this is why Hilda was having panic attacks. Why her case is hugely relevant to this book however is that in my experience, this particular chain reaction, along with the habit of control (which we will look at in Chapter 10) occurs in all panic attacks and panicky feelings.

Why it's happening really is that simple. The person who is having panic attacks is getting anxious about *being anxious*. For them, anxiety isn't just a miserable emotion. No, for people who get panic attacks, anxiety has developed a whole new dimension.

For them anxiety, instead of being something that should protect them, has become the tiger itself. A tiger, that no matter how much they try to run from, they can't escape.

So there we have it. Hilda could now see in her logical mind where she had been going wrong all these years. But that was all she could see. As she said herself: 'That's all very well and good. But what do I do the next time I panic? Because when I panic, all that good information will go out the window. When I panic I can't think, I just run.'

And I agreed with her. Because she had being running for so many years her emotional mind had the strength of a tractor whilst her logical mind had the strength of a bicycle. And no matter how hard a bicycle tries, it's never going to out-pull a tractor. So what was Hilda to do?

Well before you throw the book away, let me reassure you, the answer is a lot more straightforward than you might think. What do I mean? Well if you ask yourself this question: Why is Hilda's emotional mind the size of a tractor? Then the answer becomes apparent.

When we are in a good space in our head, or rather when we have good mental health, our logical and emotional minds are in balance with each other. That is, they are at a 50/50 balance. We call this our wise mind.

Whether we manage to keep this 50/50 balance when things get tough is determined by our behaviour. If we keep a balance in our behaviour that reflects our wise mind, then it's easier to maintain this stability.

If, though, we act in a way that reflects what our emotional mind is telling us, then we reinforce to ourselves that what our emotional mind is telling us is correct. And if we continuously keep acting in a way that reinforces what our emotional mind is telling us, then this starts to become our reality.

At this point we depart from good mental health and start drifting into mental ill health. Our emotional mind starts to dictate how we view our world. In Hilda's case, she was reinforcing to herself that anxiety was dangerous and must be avoided at all costs. So for Hilda, she had acted her way into wrong thinking.

Solving the Problem

Of course if you find that you have acted your way into the problem, then the only way to a solution is to act your way out of the problem. In Hilda's case, this meant that at some point, if she wanted to conquer her panic, she had to stop running every time it happened. She had to put my theory to the test.

Hilda had to teach her emotional mind that if she didn't run and didn't try to control the feelings, they would follow the path I've outlined in Fig 3. The panic would follow the line B in the graph in Fig. 4 and would only last a few minutes.

Why? Well if she didn't run, then her logical mind would have a chance to see in reality whether there was a danger or not and if it didn't find a real danger it would switch off the anxiety reaction. Scary, isn't it? To go against what you've been doing all this time and try something new. It's like Columbus sailing west; expecting to sail off the end of the world at any time.

The reality is that if you do try what I'm saying then, like Columbus, you will find that you don't sail off the end of the world. Instead, like Columbus you will find a new world. Except your new world will be one that is free from the panic that is currently crippling you.

The Solution

The solution then is to just give it a lash. Look around you and you will find loads of self-help books that will give you various skills to overcome your anxiety. Look at them all and find one that appeals to you.

All I'm asking is that when you look, don't pick one that says it will take the anxiety away for you without you having to do anything. Books that say they will show you a way that does not involve you having to face your anxiety are to psychotherapy what snake oil was to medicine and cowboys in the wild west.

They won't work and will probably cost you a lot of money. As I said at the start of the book, be very careful who you let into your mind. I would also add 'and your pocket'.

Overcoming emotional problems is like learning to drive

a car. You can read as many books as you like, but at some stage you've got to get behind the wheel and practise. And you don't practise by going onto the motorway the first day. No, you practise on a quiet road when there's no traffic about.

Learning CBT skills to overcome anxiety works on the same principal. Only trying it when you're having a panic attack is the therapy equivalent to taking your first driving lesson on a motorway. Try to find a mental health 'quiet road'. Find something small in your life that you can practise on. And when you do I want you to practise what we call the ABC method.

> A stands for *Activating Event* or as I've called it, the trigger.
> B stands for your *Belief*. This is what you say to yourself about the trigger.
> C stands for *Consequence*. How you felt and what you did.

Take an innocuous situation that you disturbed yourself over, like getting frustrated about something not going the way you wanted. Try to think in our terms. Look at how you felt first. This is because when you are feeling anxious, your feeling is often the first sign that something is wrong.

Next, ask yourself when you first noticed the feeling. What was happening at the time? It is important to do this, as frequently we are feeling disturbed for some time before we notice it.

Thirdly, try to figure out what you said about the event/trigger. What did you say to yourself? What was it about the initial event that you felt anxious about?

Finally, look at how you reacted to the situation. What did you do? Was it a reinforcement of what you thought emotionally?

Laboratory Exercises

Once you've got the idea it's time to try the ABC in a controlled setting. Hard as it may seem, I want you to think of triggering the anxiety.

Next I want you to think about how *strongly* you think you will feel about it. Mark the strength of how you think you will feel out of 10.

1	2	3	4	5	6	7	8	9	10
No Feeling							Feeling Strongly		

So if you feel that triggering your anxiety would be like eating your own hair, i.e. 7 out of 10, you're ready to go to the next step.

Now I want you to voluntarily put yourself into a situation where you will feel anxious. The trick is to do something that will bring you to 7 out of 10 on your anxiety scale. The idea is to do something that will set off your anxiety without overwhelming you.

Note how far you actually get before you feel 7 out of 10. Note all the sensations occurring in your body. Try to just observe the adrenaline reaction without attaching any particular relevance to it.

Now hold yourself at that point for a few minutes before withdrawing to your comfort zone. Look at how bad you rated it was going to be and compare your score to how bad it actually was. I'm sure you'll find that it wasn't as bad as you thought it was going to be.

Why is this? The fact is that when we think of something, we usually think it will be worse than what it really turns out to be. What do I mean? Well try this:

Do not think of spilling milk

When you read that, what did you think of? Most likely it was of milk spilling. And how much milk did you imagine spilling – loads of milk spilling all over the place?

Try to think up a few more of these exercises with other things that you feel disturbed about. Like the exercise above, practise doing the opposite of what you would usually do.

After a while you will start to realise at an emotional level all that I've being describing so far. When you start to realise that you can change the way you feel at an emotional level you are then ready to 'go on the motorway'.

The Core of the Solution

So now we get to the core of the solution – how to cope with the panicky feeling when it happens. The secret in doing this is to realise that if you want to overcome it then you've got to change how you're reacting behaviourally when it happens.

If you keep running and indulging in all your usual safety behaviour then you're going to keep feeling panicky. Similarly, the purpose of the exercise is not to remove that panic, but to observe what's going on so you can look at what, if any, danger is present.

So first things first, the next time you feel panicky, the worst thing you can do is try to resist it. So instead of doing this, I want you to remain wherever it is you are and just allow the physical sensations wash over you like a wave.

Observe, without trying to change anything, what physical sensations you are experiencing. Focus on the physical sensations only, not on what you think they mean.

Examine each physical sensation as it happens and focus on each in turn, keeping in mind what I've described above. Instead of just accepting that they are dangerous, look for actual dangers. You won't find any.

As the initial panic subsides, try to find as many of the

physical sensations that I described above as you can. If you're near a pen and paper, write them down. Be as comprehensive as you can.

As the panic period subsides, focus on the world around you. Look at how things have been going on as normal whilst you were observing the physical sensations.

Notice every part of everything that is going on in your field of vision. How vibrant colours are; smells that you hadn't detected before; sounds that you didn't hear before.

Over the following few minutes, your physical symptoms of panic will subside. No, you haven't died. The men in white coats haven't hauled you off and you haven't gone screaming and running all over the place. Curiously, because they're usually so wrapped up in themselves, very few people will have noticed you either.

Repeat this exercise as best you can whenever you get panicky. Don't think you have to get it all right. In my experience, you don't have to get it 100 percent right in order to get a result.

To get the result, you've just got to try a different way to the way you usually try to cope. Once you start to try what I've suggested, you have inadvertently stopped demanding that you must not get panicky. By relinquishing the demand that you must not get anxious, you are inadvertently saying to yourself at an emotional level that the symptoms are not dangerous.

And once you're convinced at an emotional level that the symptoms aren't dangerous, the panic attacks will cease to be. (You can't have a panic attack unless you attach a danger to the physical symptoms.)

You must try the exercises though; if you don't then you are not reinforcing at an emotional level what you've learned. And if you don't reinforce behaviourally then you won't remedy the panic attacks. Hilda listened to what I had to say.

She then, despite herself, did as I asked her:

'It was in the local Tesco that I made the breakthrough. It was Christmas Eve and I still had so much to get for the dinner the following day. Tesco was always as bad as the post office. I usually avoided going there for fear of having a panic attack. Today however I didn't have the luxury of avoiding it. If I didn't go in, there would be no dinner for Christmas day.

'I was in the chilled foods section when it happened. I could feel my heart starting to race and my legs get all shaky. I wanted to run, to get out of there. I could feel myself starting to panic. It was then that I suddenly realised that I was saying something completely different to myself.

'All my life I had run from fear. I couldn't allow myself the luxury of going shopping. Avoiding panic was all-consuming for me. At that moment standing in the chilled foods section I realised that now I was saying that I didn't have the luxury of the panic attack. Panic or not, I still had to do the shopping.

'The Christmas dinner was now more important than avoiding the panic. It was then I realised that even though the feelings were crap, they weren't dangerous. I hated them but I wasn't afraid of them.

'Standing there and just letting the sensations happen, I started to realise that if I just put up with them they would go of their own accord. As the sensations subsided, I realised that I was free. I had endured a panic attack without even trying to run away. I wasn't afraid of them.

'As I left the shop and headed for the car I felt myself starting to cry. This time however they were not tears of fear and pain but tears of release. I realised that I was no longer anxious about getting anxious, that my panic attacks would never again control my life. I could give my kids their Christmas. The monkey was finally off my shoulder.

'I will never forget that Christmas as long as I live. I got anxious from time to time over things like would the turkey be properly cooked. Normal stuff like that. This time though the monkey was gone. I could enjoy watching my children opening their presents eating their dinner and just being a family.

'I heard somewhere that the only things you can leave your kids are memories. Well now that I had got rid of the panic attacks, I had taken a huge step in ensuring that the ones I left them were good ones'.

Chapter 3

What Is Mental Health?

Mental health is one of those things that very few people can define, but everybody strives for. If you strive to be happy, look for rewarding and fulfilling relationships and want to be able to deal with most situations that life throws up at you, then you're looking for good mental health.

Even though there's been a lot of emphasis in recent years by the health profession to encourage good mental health, there are very few people who understand just what it is or how to create it.

One of the most fundamental mistakes people make when they think of mental health is to regard it as merely not having a mental illness. But as we will see there is a lot more to mental health than just avoiding mental illness.

Physical Health vs. Physical Illness

An easy way to differentiate between the two is to use an analogy explaining the difference between physical health and illness and then translate this to mental health.

Imagine we have two people: Paul and John. (see Fig. 5). Paul is a thirty-a-day smoker, drinks like a fish, never exercises and is three stone overweight. His weekends consist of getting plastered with his mates on Friday and Saturday nights and watching the football. As he tucks into his full Irish breakfast each morning he scoffs at people who live different lifestyles. 'There's nothing wrong with my lifestyle,' he boasts. 'Look at me, never been a day sick in my life'.

John on the other hand is a diabetic since his early teens. Even though he has diabetes, he leads an active lifestyle. Last year he ran the Dublin city marathon. He watches his weight, doesn't smoke and only drinks in moderation. He would never regard himself as a health freak, but just likes to take care of his body and not abuse it.

Two different people who are living very different lifestyles. Now having read both, ask yourself which one is the sickest? On the surface you would be forgiven for thinking that Paul was the sickest. But read it again.

Paul boasts that he has never been sick a day in his life, which is true. John on the other hand has diabetes, which is an illness. Therefore the only conclusion we can draw is that John has a recognised sickness. So theoretically he is the sickest.

But now let's look at who is the *healthiest*. Even though Paul is not sick (at the moment!) there is no way that you could describe his lifestyle as being healthy. John on the other hand leads a healthy lifestyle and can only be regarded as the healthier of the two. So when we examine both Paul and John carefully, John is physically both the sicker and the healthier of the two.

We now have the confusing situation whereby John can be described as both having a physical sickness and being healthy. This demonstrates how physical health and illness are different concepts. You can be both sick and healthy at the same time:

PAUL:

- Excessive Smoker
- Excessive Drinker
- Overweight/
  Unhealthy Diet
- Never Exercises

JOHN:

- Diabetic
- Non-Smoker
- Moderate Drinker
- Optimum Weight
- Exercises Regularly

Fig. 5: Paul & John

Mental Health vs. Mental Illness

The same thinking can be applied to mental health. To illustrate this let's take the example of Aoife and Liz (see Fig. 6).

Aoife is a workaholic. She drives herself at whatever she does and demands she is in control of everything that affects her. She is merciless on herself and views any failure to be in control as a lack of motivation or some other character flaw. This is especially true in her attitude to others. She can't abide people who settle for less than perfection. That is why she drives herself so. And there has been a big pay off in this for her. She's the boss of her own company.

As for personal relationships though, well she just hasn't found anybody who quite fits her checklist. They seem alright in the beginning but as time goes on, the more flaws she finds, and Aoife just can't abide flaws. Why can't they just think and be like me, she complains to friends over drinks after work on Friday nights.

Liz, on the other hand, spent some time in a psychiatric hospital fifteen years ago for an alcohol and drug addiction. She has been clean and sober since. She recognises the importance of avoiding drink and drugs one day at a time, but it's years since she had even a mild urge for them. She is married to Tom whom she loves for all his faults and they have two lovely children.

She learned a long time ago to not take herself or life too seriously. She strives to not 'sweat the small stuff' and succeeds at this most of the time. She has many friends and likes to keep a balance in everything she does. She is a diligent worker and has been promoted into a management position in her company. Not that she succeeds every day though. If she finds she is losing her emotional 'balance' then she has a few close friends she can talk to and this usually works to help keep things in perspective.

Now having read both of their stories, try to figure out which one is the sickest. Since Liz is a recovering alcoholic and Aoife has never been treated for mental illness then it's easy to conclude that Liz is the only one who actually has a sickness.

But now try to figure out which one is the healthiest. Even though some people may regard Aoife's lifestyle as the way to go, Liz's attitude and her mental health lifestyle is actually the healthiest.

It's true; years ago most people would have regarded a diet rich in red meat and full fat dairy produce as the healthiest diet to have. Anybody that ate Ryvita or followed a vegetarian diet was regarded as a 'crusty' complete with the image of dungarees and open sandals. Similarly a good 'healthy' tan was regarded as the epitome of healthy skin. We now know that this is not the case and that living a lifestyle like this is a sure way to an early grave. In recent years with the help of good health promotion this knowledge is now generally accepted in society.

However we also know that living a lifestyle like Aoife's not only is the most ineffective route to happiness and fulfilment, it can do immense damage to your mental health and is one of the leading causing factors behind depression and anxiety.

There is an attitude in society however that tries to sell Aoife's life as the ideal type of life. This concept of 'being in control' is presented in advertising and the media as something we must strive for.

'There's no prize for second best' we are informed in adverts for soft drinks. Of course, the inference is that if you're not 'in control' then this must be down to a lack of motivation or some other character flaw in you. Those of us who work in mental health regard trying to live by this type of philosophy as being complete nonsense. We see it as somewhat similar to the tobacco industry promoting cigarettes as the most effective way to clear phlegm from your lungs, (it does encourage you to cough, doesn't it?).

AOIFE:
• Workaholic
• Perfectionist
• Very Successful at Work
• Dissatisfied with many of her Personal Relationships

LIZ:
• Recovering Alcoholic
• Hard Worker
• Moderate Success at Work
• Very Satisfied in Personal Relationships
• Satisfied with putting her best effort into what she does

Fig. 6: Aoife & Liz

Mentally Healthy People

Therefore, what would be an accurate definition of mental health? I'd be the first to admit that trying to define it in a way that people would understand is very difficult. However, one way of illustrating mental health is to describe mentally healthy people.

Some years ago the Mental Health Association of Ireland (now Mental Health Ireland) released a small brochure where they listed the characteristics of people with good mental health. They divided these characteristics into three categories:

1. How they feel about themselves.
2. How they feel about others.
3. How they are able to cope with everyday life.

Sadly this brochure is no longer in print. I did, however, take its idea some years ago and use its concept as a questionnaire to assist people to get some kind of idea where their mental health is at and to clearly show areas where they might want or need to improve.

Have a look at the following. You will see the characteristics as a series of statements. Answer these when you're on your own first. Then ask someone who knows you well to answer them about you.

Like me, most people will find their loved ones giving a very different picture of them than they have of themselves. Most of us are like that. We would like to think of ourselves as being a certain type. Unfortunately, most of what we would like to think of ourselves, is wrapped up in pure fantasy.

Let's take a look at the characteristics of people with good mental health. Give the questionnaire a try. Don't take it too seriously though and don't feel despondent or anxious if you find that you're not doing too well in your results.

As we shall see later in the book, we're all flawed in some way or another. We can strive for good mental health, but just like physical health, we don't achieve an A+ all of the time.

In doing the questionnaire, look at each statement and mark yourself out of 10 where 1 means you're absolutely hopeless with this characteristic through to 10 in which you are a 'paragon of virtue' with it.

How I Feel About Myself

1. I don't get overwhelmed by my emotions – fear, anger, love, guilt or worries.
2. I can take life's disappointments in my stride.

3. I have a tolerant, easy-going attitude towards myself as well as others and I can laugh at myself.

4. I neither underestimate nor overestimate my abilities.

5. I accept my shortcomings.

6. I have self-respect.

7. I feel able to deal with most situations.

8. I take pleasure in simple, everyday things.

How I Feel Around Other People

1. I'm able to give love and to consider the interests of others.

2. I have personal relationships that are satisfying and lasting.

3. I like and trust others and feel that others will like and trust me.

4. I respect the many differences I find in people.

5. I do not take advantage of others, nor do I allow others take advantage of me.

6. I can feel I am part of a group.

7. I feel a sense of responsibility to fellow human beings.

How I Meet the Demands of Life

1. I do something about my problems as they arise.

2. I accept my responsibilities.

3. I shape my environment whenever possible and adjust to it whenever necessary.

4. I plan ahead and do not fear the future.

5. I welcome new experiences and ideas.

6. I make use of my talents.

7. I set realistic goals for myself.

8. I am able to make my own decisions.

9. I am satisfied with putting the best effort into what I do.

Remember, no one characteristic can define you as having good mental health. Similarly, if you're missing a few of them, it doesn't mean that you have poor mental health.

However, no matter how you did in the questionnaire, like the rest of us you can do something to improve your mental health. Remember, the better your mental health is, the better you will enjoy life and deal with all the things life throws at you.

And to improve your mental health all you have to do is cultivate these qualities. By cultivating the qualities then like physical health, small changes can get big results.

Neither do you have to do it all the time. In looking after your diet, you don't have to eat healthily all the time. Neither do you have to practise all these mental health principals all of the time. And, hey, who doesn't love to pig out with a smoked cod and chips . . . with a tub of Häagen Daz for dessert from time to time?

Remember that in order to be successful, all that is required at this stage is to be willing to grow into these principals, and to work towards getting a balance. It's a bit like going to the gym. The more you practise, the more weights you're able to lift, the faster and longer you can run and the fitter and healthier you become.

If you practise good mental health exercise, then the more you practise, the better able you'll be to live with yourself, the more you will notice an improvement in your relationships and the more you will be able to handle situations that you used to find incredibly hard to cope with.

The end result of this, of course, is that as time goes on it will take more and more to knock you off balance. But remember life, like mental health, 'is a journey, not a destination'. We will never arrive at a point where we can say we've got it. Nobody does. But as you improve your mental health the good times will get better and the bad times just won't seem to be as bad.

A nice way of grasping this at an emotional level (we call that 'conceptualising the idea') is to try this exercise. Think of people you know and admire. You can play this game with friends or on your own. It's a nice way to spend an hour. Try to visualise people you know who seem to have that something about them that you just can't put your finger on. They seem to have an emotional balance and never seem to get worked up too much about anything.

Maybe you can't think of anybody at the moment, but look around, they are all around you. They just don't make headlines and seem to be just ordinary. However there is a peace about them that you wish you had. These are people with good mental health.

So how do they do it? Before I can explain in any meaningful way that you will understand, we first have to look at where emotions come from and why we feel what we do.

Chapter 4

Why We Feel What We Do

Lynn is a woman who came to see me a few years back for depression that had been triggered by the death of her mother two years previously. Her mother had died after a long illness and Lynn had nursed her for the last few years of her life.

The last few months of her mum's life had been very difficult. After the death, friends and family continuously commented on how good and thoughtful a daughter Lynn had been, looking after her mum like that.

They said that she must have been a saint and that surely her mum was now looking down from heaven so grateful for all the care Lynn had bestowed on her.

Everybody was just so kind. They all told her that they 'understood' how devastated she must be feeling. Friends and family empathised with her, saying how they 'were both so very close. There'll be a huge void in your life now. You must feel so lonely.'

Not My Feelings

What distressed Lynn most was that she didn't feel any of this at all. Towards the end, all she could remember was praying that it would all end soon. And when her mum finally died she felt a huge sense of relief that it was all over. This sense of relief lasted all through the funeral.

Sure, she was sad that her mum had died, but the last few years had been very difficult for Lynn. At times she had felt very resentful that she had to care for her mum and put her own life on hold.

She was grateful to everyone for their kindness, but she was nowhere near as sad as she felt people expected her to be. She had tried to talk to her sister about how she felt, but stopped herself as she felt so guilty about the way she was feeling.

'How can I feel like this?' she thought. 'Surely if I had loved my mum, I would be feeling a lot sadder than I am.

'When someone you really love gets sick then you should feel totally devoted to their care and when they die you should feel totally devastated. That's what should happen.

'And if you don't feel like that then there must be something bad or wrong about you.'

The more she thought about it the more depressed she got. By the time she came to see me she had totally convinced herself that she hadn't really loved her mother at all: that she was only looking after her because of a sense of obligation and as such, must be completely disingenuous. She found it nearly impossible to reconcile this attitude with the feelings of emptiness and loneliness that she was actually feeling and was thinking that maybe this was a punishment for being such a fraud.

As I listened to her story I remember feeling more and more lost as to what to do. All I could do was ask her as gently as I could what way she thought she should have been feeling. You see, before I was ever a therapist I was a nurse for over twenty years and like all nurses had dealt with my fair share of death. I knew that the emotions Lynn had during her mum's illness and at the time of her death were not only entirely normal but also very common.

Not only can it be very difficult to watch someone you love suffer, it can be even more difficult to cope with having to carry the weight of their emotions as well as your own.

That is why it is very normal and common to find yourself wishing that the person would die. This is not a sign of uncaring, but a symptom of the stress the person is under. The more you care about someone, the harder it is to carry the cross of having to watch them die, and the quicker you may want it to be over.

I remember Lynn looking at me as if I had two heads when I asked her how she believed she should be feeling. Surely as a therapist I should know what feelings would be 'normal' to have in this kind of situation. When I admitted that I didn't know what a 'normal' emotion was, I'm sure she started to question my competency. I persevered though and gently kept challenging her as to where she had learned there was a 'correct' way to feel. That if something happened to you, that you should feel a certain way.

It's very common to see attitudes like Lynn's in my line of work. When I ask people where they think emotions come from I usually get a blank stare.

It has got to be one of the most perplexing things in the world today that even though we spend all of our lives experiencing and dealing with the fallout of our emotions, very few people can give a simple explanation as to where they come from.

Different Theories

At a talk about CBT given to a group of mental health professionals by a good friend of mine, Brian Kelly, even the experts there could not explain where emotions come from. You might think a very simple question like this would have been easy for them to answer. Not so by a long shot!

One of most common errors people make when they think of psychotherapists is that they are all the same. People have this idea that we all share a common philosophy as to what causes emotional problems.

This is not the case. Describing psychotherapists as all the same is a bit like saying that all mammals are the same. All mammals may share common characteristics, but each species is different and has evolved according to its needs and the resources at its disposal.

This is similar with psychotherapists and the way we think. Each psychotherapeutic 'modality' has its theory as to the underlying reasons that lead us to feel differently to each other. And this can cause a big problem for people. Because there are as many modalities of therapy as there are therapists, what should be a simple answer becomes very complicated once it has been filtered through each therapy's philosophy.

We will look at a number of those theories later but for the moment let's try to come up with a straightforward answer as to where emotions come from. We can do this very simply if we use some simple imagery. So let's take the example of Gerry and Tony.

Gerry & Tony

One day two friends, Gerry and Tony, were walking through the city centre. As they passed by a laneway two muggers approached them holding knives and demanding their wallets. Both Gerry and Tony were so shocked that they just handed over the wallets without thinking. The following day they met up to see how each of them were feeling about the mugging.

Gerry was very angry about what happened, but Tony

was feeling anxious. Both very understandable emotions to have, but why do you think they were feeling like this?

At first glance it would be understandable to conclude that the mugging had caused their feelings. This is a common misconception that most people make. When something happens we have a habit of thinking of how it *made* us feel. We think that when something happens, it is the event itself that has caused our reactions.

However if this was the case then surely Gerry and Tony would be feeling the same thing, which they are not. If it is true that our feelings are the result of what has happened to us then surely if the same thing happens to two separate people, they should feel the same thing. If the muggers had stabbed them both they would probably have ended up with similar physical injuries. You could say that the knife had caused the physical injury.

Many people think that the same happens in our minds. They believe that if you are mugged then you *should* be feeling a certain way, that our minds work in the same way as our bodies. This is incorrect. It is understandable why people may think this, since when certain things happen, they often have similar emotions.

Since the two lads were mugged, we regard feeling angry or anxious as normal. This is because we can identify with these feelings and a lot of people who are mugged experience them.

But what if, like Lynn, we feel something that people can't readily identify with? Then the philosophy of the circumstances causing our emotions runs into trouble. A common error many people and indeed health professionals make is that if we can't identify with an emotional reaction we view it as 'abnormal' and unfortunately this is what Lynn was doing.

Epictetus

Confused? Well don't worry. If at this stage you can just keep an open mind that events don't cause our emotions then we can explore further on what actually does.

You see, if the mugging hadn't caused Gerry's and Tony's feelings, then what had? Maybe they had reacted differently because of other factors or reasons?

This was the question that intrigued two very famous psychotherapists, Aaron Beck and Albert Ellis, in the late sixties and early seventies. Their training and backgrounds failed to provide any answers and they had become very frustrated.

Ellis himself came from a psychoanalytic background. He found that it took clients years and years to understand why they felt certain ways. And it was their frustration at the 'inefficiency' of other forms of therapy that led both Beck and Ellis back to the fundamental question of what causes us to feel what we do.

What they didn't realise at the time was that an obscure philosopher in ancient Greece called Epictetus had discovered the answer in back in the second century. Epictetus was a philosopher from the stoic school. That is, he followed the stiff upper lip attitude to life. Stand firm, etc. One day whilst pondering some aspect of life he had a startling realization that:

> People are not disturbed by things, but by the views they make of them.

Sounds very simple, doesn't it? But it is this simple concept that is the basis of *all* CBT thinking. You see, the reason Gerry and Tony were feeling differently is that they were interpreting what the mugging meant to them differently. This means that the mugging meant different things to them both.

Our Interpretation

Gerry's interpretation was 'How dare they do that to me. People like that should be strung up.' Tony, on the other hand, was thinking about how close a shave to death he had. 'God,' he thought, 'They could have killed us. This city has got too dangerous. This could happen again.'

Their emotions were determined by what they were saying to themselves about the mugging.

Light Switch Analogy

When we feel something, what actually causes the feeling is this: as we encounter a situation we set up a chain reaction of thoughts in our head. These thoughts are a bit like switching on a light.

Think about what happens when you turn on a light at night. The switch does not *cause* the light. All the switch does is connect an electrical circuit which causes a current of electricity to run up a wire.

This wire is connected to another wire, and then another until the current eventually reaches a filament in the bulb. This filament heats up, which in turn heats up a gas which emits the light. This chain reaction is instantaneous. We can't see it. As soon as you click the switch, the light comes on. This is why we say that we turn on the light when we flick the switch.

Our emotions trigger the same way. When something happens to us we interpret it. We then interpret our interpretation. We then go through a whole series of interpretations until we finally come to a conclusion as to what the event means to us.

We call this our evaluation, and it is this evaluation that

causes our emotion. To sum it up, our emotion is caused by our evaluation of our interpretation, or in other words *our conclusion about what the event means to us.*

Like the light switch however, this emotional chain reaction happens instantaneously. We don't consciously have to interpret each interpretation. The chain reaction happens almost as if it were automatic. And you don't just have chain reactions one event at a time. You can be having numerous 'chains' all at the same time.

Reality

If you want an example of this then think of this chapter the next time you're driving your car or walking somewhere. When we are on our own, we always have an internal dialogue going on in our heads. This is our brain interpreting our environment trying to make sense of our lives and the world we live in. For as we know, none of us live in reality; we live in what we perceive reality to be.

As we will see, this is very true – the same things can mean very different things to each person experiencing them. In Gerry and Tony's case the fact that they were mugged meant very different things to each of them. What things mean to you can be influenced by where you are in your life at that moment. So things you never thought about can suddenly become hugely significant as your life circumstances change.

Karen's Story

For example, Karen was a lady who once came to see me because she had developed a fear of flying. This had only manifested itself when she had children. When she was single she only had to think about herself.

'Now,' she thought, 'what will happen to my children if I'm killed?'

Her interpretation of dying had changed in that she now thought, 'It's no longer just about me.' The consequences of dying had changed what dying meant to her.

This may sound like I'm getting into psychobabble or that I'm being pedantic. However if you can just grasp that it's not the event but our interpretation of the event that causes our feelings then this understanding can have a profound effect on your life. To illustrate this profound effect, and understand how it can help, let's meet Lisa.

Lisa's Story

Lisa is a woman who came to see me some time ago. A few years previously she had been on holidays when she had got separated from her friends. Alone in a resort where she couldn't speak the language, she couldn't find her way home.

She met a local man who she had been talking to earlier in the night. He seemed nice and was concerned that she was on her own, so he offered to drive her to her apartment.

On reflection after, she recalled thinking that as the journey continued something was not quite right. The buildings were getting smaller and smaller the further he drove, going from apartment blocks to single-storey houses and eventually countryside.

As she had had a few drinks her mind was slowed down and she didn't think too much about it. It was only when he turned off the main road onto a dirt track that she realised that things were very wrong. When she challenged him she was met by a smack in the mouth and told to shut up.

He then pulled over by the side and proceeded to rape her. When he was finished, calm as you like he dropped her off at her apartment and even went so far as to kiss her on the cheek before he let her out.

Shame and Guilt

About two years later she presented to her GP with all the symptoms of depression which were a result of the shame and guilt she felt about the rape and was referred to me for help.

She had never told anyone about the rape for fear of what they would think of her. You see, she was afraid that people would view her the way she viewed herself. You may ask why she would feel ashamed and guilty considering that she was the victim. However, as with other forms of abuse, these are quite common emotions to have. As we will see later they are also feelings that cause a log jam in our heads and prevent us from coping healthily with circumstances.

Gradually Lisa allowed herself to get to know me and feeling safer, she gradually opened up about what happened. 'How could I have been so stupid to have got into the car with him?' This thought tortured her over and over again.

The flogging she gave herself over this was bad enough, but it was nothing compared to the flogging she gave herself over the rest. Lisa had herself convinced that she in some way must have been looking for it.

She was basing this on two things:

> 1. When he attacked her, she made no attempt to fight him off.
> 2. Whilst he was having sex with her, she felt herself getting 'wet down there'.

With these two pieces of information she had concluded that in some way she must have been asking for it.

Common Reactions

I started by explaining that the reason she was thinking this was because of how she was 'processing' what had happened to her. Many people who are raped think that because they have a physical sensation when the sex act is taking place that in some way they are a willing participant. This is not so.

The physical reaction of arousal is exactly that, a physical reaction to your sexual organs been stimulated and in a lot of cases is an automatic reaction which can occur without any sexual desire being present.

Lisa hadn't known this. I explained that the only way she could have been guaranteed no physical reaction was to have had a good dose of local anaesthetic into her genitalia which she clearly had not. Similarly, as your sexual organs are being stimulated, simple messages of some form of desire can be triggered in the brain. Once again, this is in no way associated with real desire or collusion of any sort.

It is very common though to see this in rape cases and it is important to correct, as it can cause untold damage if it is left unchecked. That is, the person mistakenly concludes that they in some way 'wanted' it.

We then went on to look at why she didn't fight him off. Besides the fact that he was twice the size of her, we examined why she made no attempt. As Lisa retold the events of that night, she kept remembering the windows of the car and the trees outside the window.

What he was doing was a bit of a blur, but she could remember all the details of the window and the trees. As we talked about the windows I asked her what had been going through her mind at the time.

Even though she was terrified of what was happening, some part of her mind was saying that she must survive. Survival was the other side of the window and in order to survive she had to get to where those trees were.

Becoming Clearer

As she reflected, more and more details became clear to her. She realised that during the rape, her mind was focusing on what she needed to do to survive. She needed to let him think that he was the boss. If he got what he wanted he might let her go.

That was why she said and did nothing. She let him do what he was going to do anyway, she was willing to let him have that, so that she would get what she wanted, namely survival.

Looking Again

By looking at the rape now she was able to see what really happened. She had accepted the lift because when she met him, he came across as being a very plausible gentleman.

At the time, she was on holidays and on a night out with her friends so her guard was down, but now she accepted that this was normal when you're on holiday. It wouldn't be much of a holiday if you were watching your back all the time, would it?

In order to ensure she would never make a mistake like that, it would have required her to have X-rayed everybody she met and have never trusted anyone, which is not possible if you want to live a happy life. This combined with finding herself in a vulnerable situation led to the incident.

Catching people with their guard down is how most criminals are able to do what they do. They take advantage of people's unwariness and act on it before the person has time to react. Ask anybody who has ever been mugged or had their bag stolen.

Wishful Thinking

It is very common for people, when they hear about stories like this, to respond with comments like, 'Well if I had been in that situation, I would have done such and such.'

Comments like these are nearly always wishful thinking on the part of the speaker. They are more in keeping with how they would like to think they would act, rather than how they actually would act.

Unless a situation has happened to you, then you can't relate how you would actually respond. Any fantasy ideas of how you would like to think you would react is precisely that, fantasy.

They can also be immensely damaging to the person who has actually been through the event, as by oversimplifying the situation, the victim can then blame themselves as being in some way 'weak' for reacting the way they did.

This was not the end of the story for Lisa. She still had a lot of healing to do. However what she did achieve whilst she was with me was to break the log jam. She realised that it was the situation that was abnormal, not her, nor her reactions.

The most profound thing that Lisa realised was that in order to change her feelings, it was not necessary to change the fact that the rape had happened.

Changing Our Thinking

This is how understanding that it is not the event but our interpretation of the event that causes our feelings can have a profound effect on our lives. Most people think that in order to improve their feelings they have to change the circumstances.

This is fine as long as you are in a position where you *can* change the circumstances. I will regularly see people who are in abusive relationships, or are in a job that they find they can't cope with, but for some reason or another they feel that at the moment they aren't in a position to break up ('kids are too young') or give up their job ('where will I find another one?').

In these cases where you can't change the circumstances, you *can* change the way you feel about them. And changing the way you feel can bring about a profound improvement in the way you are able to cope with it.

Remember the people we met in Chapter 1? The first thing they learned that allowed them to overcome their difficulty was this concept and it is this concept that underpins all recovery.

Changing Our Minds

So is it that difficult to change your interpretation? In reading this you're probably thinking that learning to change the way you interpret events is always very difficult and indeed many people think that they are unable to change how they view things at all.

What you probably don't realise is that you are doing it every day in every area of your life. Think of all the people you have liked or disliked over the years or attitudes you've held about certain things. Do you still feel the same about them now? Have you ever liked someone and now dislike them or vice versa?

To change the way we feel involves changing the way we interpret. It's not possible to go through life without regularly changing the way we interpret events. How many times have you told your children that they needed to change their attitude about something or other?

Understanding this concept is vital in achieving the qualities that go with good mental health. Remember the checklist in Chapter 2? One of those statements reads:

> We change situations whenever possible but adapt to them whenever necessary.

It is not possible to adapt to situations without changing our interpretation/attitude in some way. Mentally healthy people are able to do this and therefore are able to better adapt themselves to situations they find difficult or stressful.

Chapter 5

More About Emotions

Remember Kathy? She's the woman we met in Chapter 1 who was getting more and more upset about her health and the possibility that there was something wrong with her. Kathy had two problems.

Her first problem was that she was anxious that there might be something wrong with her. The second problem was that even though she knew she was being illogical in her thinking, she still couldn't stop the anxiety.

Of the two problems it was actually the second that was causing her the most distress and preventing her from dealing with the first. The second problem had to do with her attitude towards herself and the fact that she was getting anxious about something so 'stupid'. 'Why can't I just see that there's nothing wrong with me?' she despaired.

People's attitudes towards her didn't help either. Her friends would spend hours trying to convince her about how irrational she was being. Can you not just *see* that there's nothing wrong with you? And it was this not being able to 'see' that was making it worse.

Her family and friends could all see that there was nothing physically wrong with her, but she couldn't. How could this be? She knew she was an intelligent woman in every other way, but no matter how much she tried to convince herself that there was nothing wrong with her, she just couldn't accept it.

Her friends would get frustrated that she wouldn't accept what she was being told and this made her feel worse.

'I must be completely nutty to be thinking the way I do,' she thought.

This attitude of knowing our thinking to be wrong but still not being able to correct it is very common. Kathy's friends and family may have thought they were helping in trying to convince her that she wasn't ill, but by trying to convince her that her thinking was illogical they were actually making the problem worse.

In order to understand why this was, we need to backtrack a bit and look a little more at why we feel what we do. Remember, in the last chapter we learned that what causes our feelings is how we are interpreting and evaluating what's happening to us.

This is accurate as far as it goes; to get the complete picture however we have to look a bit more closely as to where emotions come from. We can then understand why, even though Kathy knew there was nothing wrong with her at one level, she was still feeling anxious.

The Lotto Analogy

I will try to explain this by using another analogy. I want you to think of doing your lotto numbers this week. You probably do this every week, but if you don't, I want you to pretend you do. The day after the draw you check your numbers and find that none of your numbers came up. How would you feel about this?

Most people wouldn't think too much about it or feel bad about it and if you're one of the millions who do the lotto every week then you've probably got plenty of experience of this. But now imagine that this week it's a special draw.

This week there is a 20 million euro jackpot for getting all six numbers but nothing for five. Once again you check your numbers and find that five of your numbers have come up. And that you were only one digit away from the sixth.

Now how would you feel? I'm sure everybody reading this would agree that they would feel more distressed, even for a short time, at missing the jackpot by one digit than six. And I would be the same. How many people would bemoan the fact that they were *so* close? I know that at the very least I'd be dining out on the story for months.

But let's look at the way we are feeling a little more closely. In the last chapter we found that how we feel is determined by how we are interpreting our experience; in this case the fact that we missed the lotto jackpot.

Now let's look at the way we are interpreting missing it by one digit. Most of us will focus on the fact we were so close, and would regard it as being reasonable to be *more* distressed about missing the jackpot by one digit than missing it by six.

Let's say though that I meet you on the street outside the shop as you exit having just found out you had missed by one digit. I point out the fact that logically, missing the jackpot by one digit is exactly the same as missing it by six. At the end of the day, you've still lost.

Do you think that at that moment I would be able to make you feel better? It's unlikely, but what if I persisted in showing you how illogical you were being in feeling bad?

Besides putting myself in jeopardy of bodily harm from you for persisting, I'm not going to help you feel any better, am I? And let's say you try to convince yourself of the same argument, you're not going to succeed in soothing yourself about the fact that you were so close.

Why do you think this is? Remember, just like Kathy you

can probably see the logic in the argument. But this doesn't help you feel better. In fact, the more logical you try to be with yourself the more logic is going to elude you. The reason why the logical argument doesn't work in this case is because the emotion isn't being processed in your logical brain.

Our Logical Mind vs. Our Emotional Mind

When something happens to us we process it in two parts of our mind. We start two interpreting 'chain reactions'. One of these is in our logical mind, but we also start an interpretation 'chain' in our emotional mind.

Our logical brain tells us that missing by one digit is the same as missing by six. However in our emotional brains we tell ourselves that it's worse. Whenever our emotional brain is in conflict with our logical brain, our emotional brain always wins out. That is why after missing the lotto by one digit we regard it as being worse.

In CBT we describe ourselves as having three minds. On the one hand we have our logical mind. This is the mind most of us would love to think we use to make all our major decisions in life and is often the one we use when giving other people advice as to what we think they should do. When used constructively our logical mind can be very useful in tackling day to day situations (see Fig. 7).

Our emotional mind is where, like the name suggests, we find our emotions. It would be a very boring and robotic life if we never felt happy, sad, love, joy etc. Similarly it would be a very dangerous world for us to live in, as our emotions are often our warning signs that all is not well.

Emotions such as hurt, anger, regret etc. are the mind's way of alerting us to the fact that there is something wrong in our world, and as we will see, it is essential in helping us to change events that are affecting us in our lives. As we go through life these two minds are in continual communication with each other.

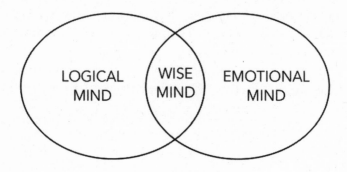

Fig. 7: 'The Wise Mind'

Finding a Balance

When we are mentally healthy we are able to find a balance between the messages we receive from these two minds and when we find this balance between our two minds we refer to this as our 'wise' mind.

Decisions made in this wise mind are usually better decisions than those made in either our logical or emotional minds. The wise mind is able to take into account how you feel about something whilst being able to 'balance' this by logically figuring out what's in your long-term best interest.

Remember the questionnaire in Chapter 2? Well look at it again and reflect on the statements that describe the 'balance' in how we feel about ourselves, how we get on with other people and how well we are able to meet the demands of life.

Finding this balance is essential to being happy, having good relationships and being able to cope with life's stressors. Keep in mind, in real life the only thing that appears in black and white is a newspaper.

Mentally healthy people are able to balance what their

emotional and logical minds tell them. That is, they make their decisions based on what their wise mind tells them *more* of the time. Note that I've said that they make *more* of their decisions based on what their wise mind says and not *all* of their decisions. This is because it is not possible to live in your wise mind all of the time.

Because we're human we all have a natural inclination to think and behave irrationally. Mentally healthy people do not think and behave rationally all the time because that's not possible. In order to be mentally healthy you only need to be *practising* it more often. And as we will see later, the most effective way of practising it is in how you behaviourally react to situations.

Finding the Balance

Being able to find a balance between the often conflicting messages that our logical and emotional minds give us is essential to living. It helps us find equilibrium between what we need versus what we want.

What's in our long-term interest as opposed to our short-term comfort? If you want an example of how important this balance is then you have to look no further than the 'healthy' way of choosing a life partner. What do I mean? Try this exercise.

Imagine your son or daughter arrives home and tells you that they have fallen in love. They tell you they want to get married next week. When you enquire as to whom their partner is, they tell you that they don't really know them.

They know that they are a habitual hard drug user and have never worked a day in their life. But they assure you that they really love them and reckon this will make everything OK. What would you make of such a decision based on what their emotional mind was telling them? Wouldn't be great, would it?

However, let's say they arrive home and say that again they want to get married. This time though they assure you that they have sussed the prospective partner out thoroughly.

They say that after being hurt so much by their ex, they decided to never put themselves into a position like that again. Their current beau is kind, thoughtful and would be very supportive. The only drawback is that they don't have any chemistry with them and are unlikely to either, as they're 'not really my type.' 'But so what,' they argue, 'they're a good catch and they love me.'

Now how would you feel about their decision to marry based solely on what they're logical mind is telling them? You could argue that their 'logical mind' decision is as bad as their 'emotional mind' one.

But now let's say they arrive home and say that they are in love with someone who they know is supportive, kind, caring, will make a good parent and spouse. What would you think of a decision like this made by combining both our emotional and logical minds? Decisions like this one, made in our wise minds, tend to be better and have more positive outcomes.

So how do we end up interpreting the way we do? Why do different people interpret differently in seemingly similar situations? Do you recall how I said that there were as many different types of therapy as there were therapists? Well, each type of therapy has its own theory as to how we end up the way we are.

Types of Therapy

It would be impossible to describe every type of therapy here, so what I will try to do is describe the major ones and try to focus on the parts of their theories that they have in common.

Constructivist theory argues that when something happens to us, we all 'construct' as many meanings as we can to it. We then use these 'constructions' to help us interpret what has happened and what it means to us.

We start these interpretation 'constructs' from our earliest moments and continue the process until the day we die and it is this process that helps us process and understand what's happening in our lives.

Systemic theory focuses on the dynamics within the family and how our interactions and relationships are all interconnected and influence the way we are. Freud once argued that no one ever forgets anything.

All our life experiences remain in our unconscious mind to further influence our future behaviour. For example, if you get hurt in a relationship, then it would be very understandable to be cautious in your next.

Integrative and humanistic theory argues that no one approach has all the answers and I agree with this. They argue that by creating a safe, respectful and nurturing environment we can all explore and change the way we are, becoming more tolerant of our life's experiences in the process.

Psychoanalytic theory believes that much of our behaviour, thoughts and attitudes are regulated by our unconscious mind and this mind is not always within our ordinary conscious control.

When psychoanalysis was first developed over a hundred years ago its theory was that by understanding our unconscious mind we could then exercise proper choice and resolve past issues.

This idea has evolved over the years and now there are many different types that focus on differing areas of our experience. Jungian theory for example looks at our immediate situations and life's problems whereas Adlerian theory looks at how our interpretation of past events can influence our present lives.

When we look at all the major psychotherapies we find that they are all basically saying the same thing. Our feelings are caused by how we interpret/construct things that happen to us and these interpretations/constructs are influenced by our life experiences.

Note however how none of them argue or suggest that it's the event itself that causes our feelings. They may all use different language to describe what happens in our heads but I think we all agree that:

> It's what we do with the event in our minds that determines how we feel.

The only real difference between all the therapies is how therapists from each modality go about helping the person to change. Each modality has its own way of achieving this change. This varies from just providing a safe, respectful environment in which you can explore your own mind to therapies that try to focus on where your thinking and attitudes came from and how they are influencing you right now.

Changing the Wheel

The trouble I have with these approaches is that whilst they will help you understand how you came to think what you think, they don't offer any solutions on *how to change* your feelings.

This is a bit like helping a person who has got a puncture in their car understand how they got the puncture and the ingredients that go into making tyres. All very well and good, but it doesn't show you how to change a wheel, does it?

And that is what CBT does. It tries not to focus too hard

on where you got the puncture; rather it focuses on giving you the skills to change a wheel. This is not to say that correcting faulty thinking from our past is not important when it's affecting our lives now.

CBT does look at past events, it just doesn't start there. CBT tries to solve the problem in the present first. We will be looking at learning how to change later but for now let's continue our journey of understanding our emotions.

Normal vs. Abnormal

A very common question that I regularly get asked is 'are all emotions normal?' Well the devil is in the detail when you try to answer that one as there is no such thing as a normal emotion, or I should say, there's no such thing as an abnormal one.

As I explained to Kathy when we met, we have absolutely no control over thoughts that enter our heads or the emotions that go with them.

If you want an example of this then try this exercise. For the rest of the day you are not to think of pink elephants. If you do think of pink elephants then you have to give your significant other one euro every time you do. Now try to get the thought out of your head. Not that easy, is it? The harder you try the harder it is to stop thinking of them.

However, whilst you may not have control over the thoughts and emotions coming into your head, you do have power over what you do with them. And what you do with them will determine how they will affect you both in the short and long term.

As we have seen, our emotions are our minds' reactions to events that occur in our lives, and whilst there is no such thing as an abnormal emotion this doesn't mean that all emotions are healthy.

So what's the difference between healthy and unhealthy emotions? If we don't describe them as normal and abnormal then how do we differentiate between the ones that are beneficial to us and the ones that are not? To do this let's use a very simple method to try to classify emotions. First let's classify emotions as positive and negative.

Positive emotions like love, joy or pleasure need very little explanation here. They are what makes life worth living and what most of us strive for. On the other side of the balance sheet however we have what we can describe as *negative emotions*.

These are the emotions that most of us would rather avoid. Emotions such as sadness, anger, hurt, that we experience at various times in our lives and as we shall see are essential to living.

Healthy vs. Unhealthy

In looking at negative emotions though, we need to further classify them into healthy negative emotions and unhealthy negative emotions. In Fig. 8 I have listed some of the most common ones. You will see from the list that with each emotion there is a healthy and an unhealthy version of it, e.g. sadness versus depression.

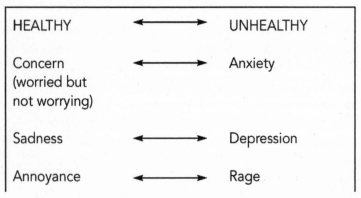

HEALTHY	⟷	UNHEALTHY
Concern (worried but not worrying)	⟷	Anxiety
Sadness	⟷	Depression
Annoyance	⟷	Rage

continued overleaf

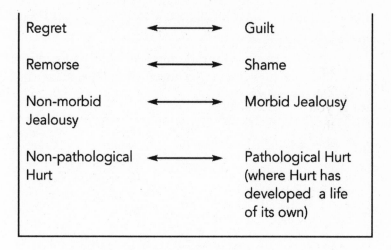

Regret	←——————→	Guilt
Remorse	←——————→	Shame
Non-morbid Jealousy	←——————→	Morbid Jealousy
Non-pathological Hurt	←——————→	Pathological Hurt (where Hurt has developed a life of its own)

Fig. 8: Healthy and Unhealthy Negative Emotions

Dr Paul Gannon is an Occupational Health doctor working in County Kilkenny. As he describes it, the easy way in defining whether an emotion is healthy or unhealthy is by looking at the effect the emotion is going to have on your ability to cope with what's happening in your life.

Paul describes *healthy negative emotions* as those emotions that are:

- Empowering, they help us change things we need to change.
- Problem-solving.
- Self-limiting, in that they fade over time when they have served their purpose.

The net effect of this is that they alert us to the fact that there is something wrong with our world and they help us identify helpful responses that will help us deal effectively with the problem.

For example, let's say that you feel angry that a work colleague is persistently late in the mornings so much so that you have to cover for them which is jeopardising your position in the company.

The healthy anger you may feel will help you confront them about their behaviour and hopefully get them to change it, thereby protecting your job.

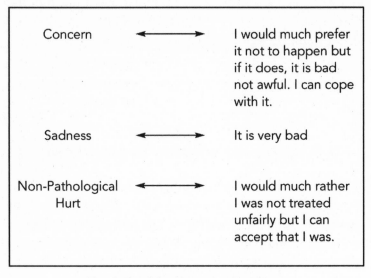

Concern	←——————→	I would much prefer it not to happen but if it does, it is bad not awful. I can cope with it.
Sadness	←——————→	It is very bad
Non-Pathological Hurt	←——————→	I would much rather I was not treated unfairly but I can accept that I was.

Fig. 9: Healthy Negative Emotions

However when we come to look at *unhealthy negative emotions* Paul similarly describes these emotions as being:

- Disempowering, they prevent us from dealing with the problem.
- Problem generating, they only make the problem worse and have a habit of creating other problems.
- Self-Perpetuating, they have a habit of remaining and continuously disabling us again and again over time.

Unlike the healthy negative emotions, they don't help us

cope. Rather they prevent us from adapting to situations. For example imagine you become enraged at your colleague's behaviour.

In this case you're liable to overreact in a way that is likely to get you into trouble. In a similar vein, getting anxious as opposed to being concerned about something is like trying to solve a maths problem by chewing bubble gum. It takes up a lot of energy but does nothing to solve the problem.

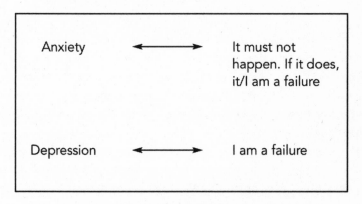

Fig. 10: Unhealthy Negative Emotions

In the next chapter, we will look at where unhealthy emotions come from and why in some instances we can have a healthy emotion. We will also look at why for some 'inexplicable' reason we invariably end up triggering the unhealthy ones from time to time.

Chapter 6

The Big MACS

We ended the last chapter with the intriguing question: what determines whether we have a healthy or unhealthy negative emotional response to something? Why is it that sometimes we are able to adapt and cope well with some things but with other things, despite our efforts, certain events just seem to 'push our buttons?'

Why is this? Well if you take some time out and look a bit more closely at what pushes your buttons, you may just find something quite startling. You see for most of us, it's not the big things that happen in our average day that push our buttons, but rather a succession of small things that upset us the most.

And to make matters worse, many people believe that because they should be able to overcome small things, they then become very frustrated and even anxious when they find that they can't.

Little Things Cause Big Problems

One of the main reasons for this is because we're human and as humans we have a tendency to oversimplify how difficult 'little' things can be to overcome.

Adopting the philosophy that 'little things should be easy'

to control and that 'big things should be very difficult', can be incredibly damaging to our mental health. It's also usually incorrect and can cause great difficulty when you try to solve the problem as it results in you looking for the problem in the wrong place.

It must be one of the biggest myths in people's perception of psychotherapy, that if you need to seek help it is because something big has happened to you and that it is this big thing that has caused your current problem. This premise is based on the incorrect assumption that big emotional disturbance is always caused by big events.

Granted, I've seen a number of people over the years that would fit into this category. We call big events like these 'critical incidents' and yes, they can influence the way we view our world. However, even though the term 'critical incident' brings up all kinds of dramatic images, in CBT the term usually refers to something much more mundane.

You see, by far the most common issues that drive people in my door are not the big critical incidents that have happened in their lives. Rather it's a succession of small incidents that has made their life circumstances critical.

These small things that can make such a huge difference to our mental health can sometimes be so small and seemingly insignificant that we're not even aware that they are affecting us so. All we notice is that we're feeling bad, but because we can't identify a significant enough 'critical incident' that would explain why, we end up lost in trying to understand why we're feeling the way we are.

Bringing the Problem into Focus

When people meet me for the first time, their thinking is usually so jumbled in their heads that they are unable to decipher what the real problem is. Therefore my initial task is to try to bring the problem into focus.

To do this I ask the person to try to describe why they have come to see me. Whilst they are doing this I try to single out as many little triggers as I can that might be feeding the problem.

Starting with simple questions like 'What do you feel depressed/anxious about?' the client and I can begin the process of helping the client find their solution.

Now you may think that asking a fairly straightforward question like this would result in a straightforward answer. Not so. You see, when I ask this, most people try to find some particular thing they feel would be appropriate to be depressed or anxious about.

When they can't find a suitable answer that would make sense to them, they respond that they either don't know or can't think of anything that they feel depressed about.

At this point I usually stop them. Instead of trying to focus on trying to find *one* reason why they are feeling the way they are, I get them to look at *everything* that is going on in their lives at that moment that is triggering their distress.

Drawing up a 'menu' of what's going on with them can be very useful in helping put some structure on their thinking and can build up a picture of the content of their lives at that point in time.

The main benefit in adopting this approach is that it starts to bring the problem into focus for the person and in doing so makes it easier to show them that quite often it's not their thinking on *one* thing that's disturbing them. Rather, it's a combination of 'faulty thinking' in relation to a lot of things that has them feeling the way they are and it's a succession of little events like these that are triggering their thinking 'chain reactions'.

However, even though there may be quite a number of thinking 'chain reactions' going on at the same time, people usually find that they invariably end up triggering the same emotions. In order to understand why this is so, let's look a little deeper into our understanding of what causes us to feel what we feel.

Now remember, up to now we have learned:

> 1. That what we feel is not caused by what happens to us but by our interpretation of what has happened to us.
> 2. That this interpretation is happening in a part of our brain (emotional brain) that believes that missing the lotto by one digit is worse than missing it by six.
> 3. That when we have interpreted what has happened to us, we come to a conclusion/evaluation about what the event means to us.
> 4. And it is this evaluation that causes our emotion.

For this chapter we are going to look further at the evaluations and conclusions we attach to things that are happening in our lives, because it is these evaluations that underpin our philosophies for living and usually are the guiding influences in how we feel and subsequently respond to things that happen in our lives.

As we apply this insight into the five habits that make us unhappy we will find that it is these underlying philosophies for living and our subsequent reactions that buttress and perpetuate our unhappiness.

Underlying Beliefs

Healthy or unhealthy negative emotional responses to events in your life will be determined by these evaluations. In CBT we call these evaluations *beliefs* and it is these beliefs that we will look at now. Understanding the particular nature of these beliefs is the secret to understanding our unhelpful emotions and learning how to change them.

Albert Ellis was a great man for cutting through the psychobabble in psychotherapy, and helping to facilitate our understanding of why we feel what we do.

He figured out that when we experience certain emotions like anxiety we are saying certain things to ourselves. He also discovered that there are certain 'evaluations' that we make that always underpin the same emotions.

This simplifies our search for understanding enormously because as Ellis found, when you strip away the superficial layers of our various personalities that differentiate us, we aren't all that different from each other at all. And not only are we not all that different from each other but we all have the propensity to make the same evaluations about what we think reality is.

It is my experience over twenty-nine years that as humans we all have a habit of making five basic errors in our thinking. It is these five errors that underpin most of the difficulties that people experience in trying to be mentally healthy and happy.

So if you find happiness and contentment eluding you no matter how many self-help books you read then it's probably for one of these five reasons.

Cognitive Dynamics

Before we can explore what I mean by that statement though, we need to look more closely at these evaluations/conclusions that Ellis described as unhealthy.

For example, people who are depressed have a tendency to conclude that because of certain reasons that make sense to them, they are failures for one reason or another and it is this view that 'I am a failure' that is the 'thinking' part that underpins depression.

We call these 'thinking' evaluations and conclusions

'Cognitive Dynamics'. Cognitive refers to the way we interpret our environment in our minds and each unhealthy negative emotion has a unique cognitive (thinking) dynamic that causes the emotion.

If you look at Fig. 10 you will see I have listed the thinking dynamic that is behind some of the more common healthy negative emotions that we all experience. These are the healthy emotions that my colleague Dr Paul Gannon describes in Chapter 4 as empowering us to solve problems.

Have a look at the list. Note the thinking/attitude style that is characteristic of the cognitive dynamic. If you look carefully you will see that what all these healthy negative emotions have in common is that they are based on beliefs that are dependent on a *non-demanding philosophy of life*.

This non-demanding philosophy concludes that whilst we may have a very strong preference for things to be the way we want them to be, we can accept that our wishes may not always come true.

These healthy emotional philosophies help in motivating us to achieve our goal as long as there's a reasonable chance we will get what we are striving for. However what these emotions also help us to do is to 'give up the chase' if the cost of the chase is greater than the payoff of the result.

Have a look at the mental health questionnaire in Chapter 2. Look at the statement again that states: *We change circumstances whenever possible, but adapt to them whenever necessary*.

Now let's look at how these attitude styles differ when we start experiencing the unhealthy negative emotions. Look at Fig. 9. Now remember, unhealthy negative emotions disempower us to solve problems.

They also end up creating more problems for us. Whilst the healthy emotion goes away when it has done its job, the unhealthy emotion keeps being retriggered even though the original event has long gone into history.

Ellis discovered that people who are feeling unhealthy negative emotions like rage, anxiety and depression aren't living by a non-demanding philosophy. Rather, people who are experiencing these types of emotions are going to much greater extremes in what they are saying to themselves.

He argued that when we have these unhealthy negative emotions, we all have certain evaluations in common that underpin our disturbance and in keeping with his philosophy of keeping it simple he called these common denominator evaluations *Big MACS*.

The Big MACS

So let's look at what Ellis meant by Big MACS. Don't worry if you don't understand the following explanations fully. You will find practical examples that will show how it all works throughout the book that will illustrate clearly what I mean.

For now just try to grasp the fundamentals of what we call the Big MACS.

The MACS in Big MACS stands for:

- M = Musts
- A = Awful
- C = Can't stand it
- S = Self or other downing

M is for MUSTS

This refers to absolute demands that we make over things. In 'must' we demand that things *must* be the way we demand them to be! This is very different to having a 'very strong preference'.

With preferences there is some degree of compromise and acceptance, however small, that things may not be the way we want them to be. Not so with *must* where there is *no* compromise. We demand that things absolutely *must* be the way we want them to be.

We all do this in a lot of ways. I may demand that I must have what I want and as long as I can satisfy my demand then there is no problem for me. (My subsequent behaviour may cause a problem for others, but that's another story.)

Musts will not cause us to have an unhealthy negative emotion as long as they are satisfied. But what if you're not able to satisfy the demand no matter how much you try or if satisfying your demands is not possible.

Making Demands

To illustrate this let's look at the dynamics of road rage. Let us say that we demand that people *must* drive the way we think they should. The consequence of this is that we are going to get ourselves worked up into a rage every time we go on the road as people will drive the way they are going to drive regardless of how we feel about it.

Furthermore, if we don't learn how to change our must then we are liable to behave in a way that will have serious consequences for us, e.g. becoming violent and ending up in court, but this still won't change people's driving habits one bit. In this case demanding has not got you what you want; it has just created a big problem.

These are extreme examples of where *must*ing can get us, but the habit of *must*ing is intrinsic in us all. Our demands crop up in all our lives. We demand that our partners *must* be the way we want them to be or do what we think they should do.

If you are in a relationship then you're probably not even aware that you demand so much. However when demanding like this becomes unreasonable, it can do untold damage in our relationships.

There is a wry relationship therapy joke that says that most people spend the first ten years of marriage trying to change their partner, and the next ten years complaining that their partner is just not the same person they married!

As a wedding present my best friend got my wife Mei and I a voucher for a course in 'Love and Marriage' (my friend knows what my wife and I are like). The course ran one night a week over six weeks and on the first night we were given an exercise. For the duration of the course, we were challenged to *make no demands on your partner and let love flourish*.

The next six weeks have got to rank as the longest six weeks I've ever lived. I would love to be able to say that I did as I was told, made no demands on my wife and gained a huge positive emotional insight in to the whole nature of love, but I can't.

I did get a huge emotional insight, but it was more in the realm of realising how much I *do* demand of those close to me and how much I do it. I found that every time I got irritated or annoyed it was because I was making some demand or other on my poor wife.

And this was not all, because the other enlightening realisation I had was that it was not the big things that I demanded must or must not be, it was loads of little things. The kind of things, that in the greater scheme of life would be quite irrelevant, suddenly achieved a relevancy that far outweighed their importance. And as if this wasn't bad enough, I also started to realise how many people demand of me as much as I do of them.

My brother Niall used to joke that people were always telling him that he needed to do this and do that. His problem however was that when left to his own devices, he didn't think he needed to do anything at all!

We all do it. We demand that we must do this and we must have that. That people must behave in a way that we believe they should. And one of the interesting characteristics about demanding is that the more we demand and get what we want the more this feeds our *demandingness*, so we demand more and more over less and less.

Priorities

When I worked as a nurse I was a Clinical Nurse Specialist in Critical Care. This meant that I worked quite a lot in Accident and Emergency units, Intensive Care and Coronary Care units. One of the most valuable experiences I took from this part of my career can be illustrated by an event that happened one night in a CCU where I was working in New York City.

Aaron was admitted to the ward as I was beginning the night shift. He had been admitted to the Coronary Care Unit via the Emergency Room with a heart attack. As I was going about my work I noticed him sitting in the bed looking very scared.

Considering that he was in hospital this was very understandable. In CCUs this fear is doubly understandable and something we often see. Heart attacks are quite often sudden and the drama of the Emergency Room is so fast moving that the person doesn't have time to think.

It's later in the CCU during the quiet hours of the night that feelings start to manifest. So Aaron's fear would have been something that I would have been sensitive to when he was admitted. As soon as I had a chance I sat down beside him and we started to chat. One of the most rewarding things about nursing is that people will share with you their most intimate secrets. And trust me; it is truly an honour when people see you as someone whom they can trust to talk to.

Aaron talked about his fears about what had happened and what the future held for him now. We spoke about his wife and young children and how they would cope if he died.

We spoke about all the monitors that were attached to him and the treatment he would be receiving for the foreseeable future. However the thing that stands out most in my mind about Aaron was what he said as we were coming to the end of my shift.

The sun had just risen over the New York City skyline and as we were on the twenty-fifth floor we had a wonderful view of it. I was busy getting things ready for the day shift when he called me over to thank me for talking to him over the night.

As he looked out the window at the skyline he remarked: 'You know, Enda, yesterday, when I saw this view, all I could think of was what my priorities for that day were. There were so many things that I was stressing myself over. What route would I take to avoid the traffic? Would I be on time for the sales meeting and would my targets be OK? Well, this morning I find I have a whole new range of priorities to think about'.

Realisations like the one that Aaron had that morning are regular occurrences in CCUs. We all fret about little things every day. However you can be guaranteed one thing about a 'visit' to a Coronary Care Unit; you may come in with one set of priorities, but you'll go out with a whole new one.

GROW has a wonderful way of putting it. 'We need to accept being discontent in lesser things, in order to be content in greater things, so we learn to be content to be discontent in many things.'

Living your life according to a *must*ing philosophy will make it nearly impossible to put this into practice.

A is for AWFUL

So why do we demand that things must be the way we think

they should be. Most of the time we demand like this because for us the consequences of our demands not being met are *awful*.

Now, the word 'awful' is fairly self-explanatory. But let's look at what Ellis meant by awful.

When I was doing my final assessments to qualify as a Cognitive Behavioural Therapist, we were given an essay to do on 'There is nothing awful in the universe. Discuss.' Jeez, what a topic to be given as an essay!

The purpose of the essay was to try and reinforce the understanding that no matter what you think is the most awful thing that may happen, there is always something worse that may happen.

At a surface level, Ellis argued that by '*awful*ising' you are reinforcing that whatever it is you are experiencing is so bad that it must not happen. So where does believing this get us?

Now you could argue that certain things are awful and it's reasonable to dread them. For example, I would dread it if my family were wiped out in a crash. And who would blame me for thinking like that?

However when people think of something as being awful, it is rare that they will have processed what is happening to them to the extent that there is 'Nothing awful in the universe.'

You see, whilst we all have ideas in our heads about what would be awful for us if it happened, most of the things we awfulise about are not the big things that can happen, but the small.

Neither do we really investigate in our heads why it would be so awful. We just accept that it would. And the consequence of awfulising is that you end up spending all of your time demanding that it must not happen, which unfortunately, rarely prevents it from happening.

All your demanding does is make you anxious, and as we

have seen, anxiety prevents you from finding a solution. The net result is, the more you awfulise, the more anxious you get. And the more anxious you get, the less able you are to find a solution since all your mental energy is focused on how awful it is.

To illustrate what I mean, let's take a case history. I want you to meet David, who was a client of mine and was an excellent example of where awfulising can get you.

David's Story

David was the CEO of a big multinational firm. Being the CEO meant that every buck stopped with him as he was ultimately responsible for everything that happened in his company.

The results of how the company was doing would have to be presented to the board of directors every three months, hence the term quarter end. At the end of each quarter year, David would have to face the board and have his performance examined.

This wasn't a problem in the early years of his career. 'All part of the job,' he thought. The problem was, though, that as he got older, it was gradually getting harder and harder to just maintain the target and keep his results adequate. Like a mouse on the wheel, he was having to run harder and faster each quarter just to remain stationary.

Furthermore, there were a number of people working under him that were just waiting for a chance to knock him off his perch and take the top job. One bad quarter end result and wham, he'd be fired. By the time David got to see me he was in crisis due to the pressure he was under. 'How much longer can I put up with this?' he used to think.

Starting the Therapy

At our initial meeting David told me that he lived in dread each day of losing his job. When I thought it would be safe to ask the question, I gently enquired had he ever figured out precisely what he would do if he *was* fired.

David looked at me aghast. How could I even think that? The thought of losing his job to him would be so catastrophic that he hadn't even dared to let himself think of it.

Not very clever, was it? Surely if you think you may lose your job, the wisest thing would be to have a few backup plans up your sleeve. Not so with poor David.

Because losing his job would be so bad for him, he spent all his energy worrying about it instead of coming up with a game plan as to what to do if it happened.

The consequence of all this anxiety was that when he got anxious, he would *catastrophise* the consequences in his head. This wasn't just fear, this was real anxiety.

Fear vs. Anxiety

The difference between fear and anxiety is that fear is usually about something that has already happened and we are afraid of it happening again.

Anxiety on the other hand is invariably about something that hasn't happened yet. And because it hasn't happened yet, we tend to overplay the consequences of it happening in our emotional mind.

A nice way of differentiating between the two is to ask oneself:

'Are you worried or are you worrying?'

If you answer *worrying* then you mean *anxious*. And the more anxious you get, the more you will catastrophise/ awfulise the consequences in your head.

There is an old expression that says: *Anxiety is the interest paid on a non-existent loan*. This is very true and if you want a small exercise that will illustrate how anxiety affects our minds then try this . . .

Do not think of spilling milk

Now, when you read 'do not think of spilling milk', what image flashed across your mind? Ten to one the image of spilling milk flashed across it. And I would bet that it was not just a small drop of milk spilling but the entire carton spreading across the floor, under the fridge, etc.

The image of a lot of milk spilling is an innocent example of how your emotional mind can work overtime. In David's case however, because he was constantly trying to put the thought of being fired out of his mind, it wasn't just a carton spilling that went through his head but a tanker full. This meant that he was unable to keep the consequences of losing his job in perspective.

David was awfulising so much that it took some time before he could persuade his emotional mind that acknowledging the fact that it could happen did not mean that we were tempting fate or some other such rot.

Once he had achieved this, we were able to start looking at what the likely consequences of him losing his job would be. David took some time out to look at this with his wife and to look at possible options if it did happen. We call this making a survival plan.

The Survival Plan

Coming up with a survival plan in situations like this has two benefits. The first is that by openly discussing the *awful* scenario, it brings the problem from the emotional mind into the logical mind.

By drawing the problem into our logical mind, this has the effect of helping to de-catastrophise the situation. Remember, when we visualise an awful situation while we feel anxious we will always visualise it in a worse light than it can ever be in reality.

The second payoff in drawing up a survival plan is to reinforce the idea that there are always alternatives. Recognising the existence of survival strategies can have a major calming effect on us.

Tacitus was a Roman general who once said: 'Better to stand and face one's share of ills, than to hide and be always fearful of what may happen.'

Sleep Disturbance

If you look at your own life you will find loads of examples of where you 'must' and 'awfulise'. Try the challenge we were given in our pre-marriage course about not making demands of your partner and you won't be long in finding a handful.

One place where I find people 'awfulising' regularly is in the whole area of Sleep Disturbance. When people find it hard to sleep, they usually make the error of trying to correct it by demanding *I must* sleep. Of course this is like demanding that you must get a song out of your head; the more you demand it, the harder it will be.

The two dynamics of musting and awfulising create havoc when we try to solve life's problems and we will see how this happens as we look at the habits. But we still have the C and the S from the *Big MACS* to look at.

So let's continue our journey into understanding why we feel what we feel, because in the next chapter we will look at the C which stands for *I can't stand it*.

Chapter 7

I Can't Stand It

When you're feeling upset, have you ever felt like stomping your feet on the ground because things are not the way you want them to be? If like most of us you have felt like this from time to time then you've been experiencing a bad dose of the *I can't stand its*.

The *I can't stand it* of the Big MACS has got to be the most subtle of all the Big MACS. It quietly lies in the long grass until it's triggered and then wham, it jumps up and bites you in the ass.

Or to be more accurate, when you experience it you jump up and bite someone else in the ass! What do I mean? This little exercise will show you.

Over the next few days just become more aware of your emotions. What you're looking for is an uncomfortable feeling that will occur when you experience something you don't like.

It may be one of your kids leaving their toys on the floor, somebody driving too slowly on the road and holding you up, or something else that you find irritating. Now ask yourself, what is it about that situation that you find most irritating? It will probably be that you're demanding that the situation must not be the way it is. So far so good, but now take your thinking a little bit further.

Look at your must more closely and ask yourself this question: 'What is disturbing me more? The situation or how I'm feeling about it?'

Most people will initially say that it's the situation, but when you act to change the situation ask yourself, 'What's the main purpose of my behaviour? Is it to change the situation or to alleviate the feeling that I'm having towards it?'

Try asking yourself this the next time you fly off the handle about something. 'Why did I blow my fuse? Was it because I just couldn't stand the situation being the way it was. Was it the situation or that I couldn't stand it?'

If the situation was one of those day to day irritants that we all experience, then your behaviour's purpose was probably to remove the feeling that you were experiencing towards the situation, i.e. I can't stand it.

Low Frustration Tolerance

We call our ability to cope with these irritants our 'frustration tolerance ability' or if you want to get *really* technical, our 'emotional regulation skills quotient'. When a person comes looking for help this is one of the things that therapists look at.

We all get upset about a myriad of things. You can recognise it fairly easily. When you feel exasperated, infuriated, perturbed or just plain frustrated about something then you're most likely experiencing our friend *I can't stand it.*

There's nothing abnormal with getting upset about something even if you think you're daft to be upset about it. We all have our irrational belief 'buttons' that can be pressed from time to time. Most of them don't do us too much harm; they are just part of who we are. Whether they will cause you a problem or not will be determined by how upset you get and how well you are able to 'self-sooth' yourself when you do.

Part of my work is training health professionals in CBT skills that they can use in their own clinical practice. There's an old saying that says that if you want to train to be a CBT therapist then undergo CBT and if you want to undergo CBT then train as a therapist. There isn't much difference between the two.

It is well recognised that in order to be able to understand someone else's mind we should first get to understand our own and the easiest way of doing this is to start looking at our own Big MACS and how difficult they can be to shift.

To do this I try to get participants in the class to do certain exercises that will trigger their own irrational beliefs and help them experience their own Big MACS in an amusing way that illustrates that we all have them.

We call this experiential learning. Remember, underneath the superficial aspects of our character, we are all very similar. We all have a tendency to make the same 'cognitive (thinking) connections' about events.

Of course, understanding this tendency makes it a lot easier to think up various exercises that will help reinforce certain CBT concepts.

Keeping It Simple

So now is as good a time as any to try a few of these exercises yourself and to look at how similar most of us are to each other. To do this I want you to think of something that frustrates you regularly. Continue on reading when you have one in your mind.

Got one? OK now ask yourself: why does this bother me so much? By asking yourself this question, you've just started the process of understanding what makes you tick, why you think as you do and how you evaluate what's going on around you. So it's worth pondering the question for a while.

After you have pondered it for a while, you will find

yourself achieving the first goal of the exercise. You see, by the time you have got this far you'll probably have found yourself doing one of two things:

1. Getting stuck for an answer fairly rapidly.

or

2. You found your mind started wandering, thinking of all the more important things you had to focus on that day.

Don't be discouraged. We're all like that. Most of us rarely ask ourselves in any great depth why we feel what we do. We just *do*. There are other reasons why you will have tended to have wandered off in your mind.

It's because you're human. And because you're human you share three unhealthy characteristics with the rest of us.

You see, as humans we are all:

- Talented avoiders
- Procrastinators (Which is laziness spelt with five syllables)
- Short-range hedonists. That is we consistently put our short-term comfort ahead of our long-term interest.

And as you've just found out, we really practise these characteristics at every opportunity. Not only that but very few of us will give up these or indeed any of our irrational philosophies and behaviours as long as there is any chance we will make them win for us.

This is why, when you read a self-help book like this, that's as far as you get – *reading it*.

Very few of us will put in the consistent work that is required to change as long as the price we're paying to keep our irrational philosophies isn't too great.

So when people look for help from people like me, it's because they have found that the cost of doing things the way they do has gotten too high, that is, it has become too painful, and the payoff is too low. Only then will most of us try the 'persistent path' to removing them.

Learning To Change

You've probably heard the saying. How do you eat an elephant? Well you don't do it in one bite. The only way you can ever hope to eat an elephant is by eating it one chunk at a time.

And don't think that you have to change everything about yourself in order to get a result. You don't. It's an amazing fact of life that small efforts can bring about big results.

As we will see in the chapter on *making the change*, you don't start the process of change by starting to change the big things in your life. You start by changing a few simple things first. Only when your 'mental fitness' level improves will you be able to attempt more difficult exercises.

Think about it logically. If you don't have the mental health skills to change some of the simpler things in your life, then you won't have the skills to be able to change and adapt effectively when something more significant needs to be changed.

So if you decide to try the following exercise, pick something simple and just give it a lash. You won't do it perfectly, but then you don't need to.

In order to be successful at it, all you've got to do is try! And by the simple fact of trying something new, you've already taken a big step towards removing the big MAC of *must* out of part of your life.

So, here goes.

Doing the Exercise

Take a preferably simple situation that regularly gets on your nerves. One of those situations that you go to great lengths to change but like groundhog day, it keeps happening.

Try to pick one that happens most days – if you pick something that only happens infrequently, you may have quite a wait before you can do the exercise.

Examples of what I mean are:

- Your partner indulges in one of their irritating habits
- Your teenager's room is in a mess
- Your friend is persistently late for lunch dates

Now, over the next two weeks, try to put yourself in the situation as much as possible. Don't focus on how you feel. You will feel narky about it. But every time the situation happens, you give yourself a treat – one that you always love.

However in this instance you are only allowed the treat *if* the situation happens. Try not to focus on your emotions, just 'do it'. At the end of the two weeks, look at your feelings. Chances are that you won't be half as bothered by the situation as before. To illustrate this, let's meet a few people who this happened for.

Áine's Story

Áine was a health professional who was on one of my courses. She was also a full-time mum who spent most of her waking hours juggling family, her job and a million other things in her life.

When I asked the class to come up with something that frustrated them, Áine was the first to come up with an example. 'Oh that's no problem finding something that ticks me off,' she said.

She then proceeded in a very humorous way to tell us about her daughter and how she was continuously at logger-heads with her over 'blaring' music in her room. No matter how she tried to confront her, she could never succeed in getting her to turn the volume down.

Every day her daughter would come home from school, head upstairs and on would go the music. Áine would follow her upstairs, bang on the door and make her turn the music down. However by the time Áine arrived back downstairs, she would hear the music slowly being cranked up again.

When I asked Áine why it bothered her so much, she didn't know. It just did. And she couldn't see how that was going to change. No prizes for guessing who was going to be the Low Frustration Tolerance exercise subject in that class.

The task was set. Every time her daughter's music blared, Áine was going to get a euro from the other nine people in the class. All she had to do was keep the tally; her mouth shut; and in the famous lines in the Tina Turner song, 'keep her mind on the money, and her eye on the wall.'

We met as a class two weeks later. The entire buzz was about how Áine had fared. I wasn't going to get very far with the lesson until we found out what had happened so we started the day off a wee bit of debriefing.

Áine started by telling us what happened from the beginning. She was motivated and eager to face the challenge. Her motivation wasn't long evaporating though when her daughter came home and went straight up to her room. Up went the music, out went the motivation.

'Oh God, how am I going to cope with two weeks of this,' she thought. She decided to persist though. As she told us later, the only thing that would be worse than the exercise would be arriving into class in two weeks' time and telling everyone that she hadn't completed the task.

The situation continued throughout the week. In came the

daughter only to clump up the stairs and bang her bedroom door shut. There followed a one minute pause, when Áine would brace herself for the onslaught, and bam, the music would reverberate against the walls.

This went on each day, but strangely as the week progressed, Áine told us, for some reason she started to get used to it. She was still frustrated but it wasn't nearly as bad as at the start of the week. It was during the second week however that Áine made a realisation that changed her whole perspective on the volume of the music.

Áine realised one day whilst listening to the racket that the day would come, sooner rather than later, when there would be *no* music coming from the room. She realised that the day would come when there would be no one at home to play music. Her daughter would grow up and leave home. 'And I don't want to see that day come,' she said.

You could have heard a pin drop in the room. Most of the class had teenage children. They all had situations like Áine's with their children. That was why they found it so funny two weeks previously. Now they all realised that the day would come when their children would all leave home, and they would no longer be exposed to their 'irritant'.

But how many wanted that day to come? How many times had they wanted to simply escape their children's irritating behaviour without thinking it through?

It was a wise person who once said: Be careful what you wish for, you might just get it!

When we allow our low frustration tolerances to flourish unchecked, and keep nourishing them with our behaviour, then like Áine we lose our ability to keep these situations in perspective at all.

Unable To Solve the Problem

When you cannot keep a rein on your frustrations, you are

liable to lose perspective on your problems. But losing our ability to keep things in perspective is only one consequence. You see, not keeping a rein also prevents you from identifying solutions to the actual problem itself. To illustrate this, let's meet Celine.

Celine's Story

Celine was another participant in one of my classes. Her situation was similar to Áine's, except that in Celine's case it was her daughter's annoying habit of pinching the shampoo from the en suite shower in Celine's bathroom.

'The story is always the same,' she said. In she would pop to the shower, forgetting to check that the shampoo and everything else was there. She would only realise when her hair was wet and she was left groping around the shower tray thinking, 'They've done it again!'

She would then start the ritual of shouting, from the shower, to the family downstairs, in the hope that someone would hear her and get the shampoo from the main bathroom.

Of course, nobody would hear her and she'd then have to complete the ritual of having to turn off the shower, find the towel and drip her way across the landing to the main bathroom to retrieve her shampoo.

Celine had often fantasised about chaining it to the shower and in her wilder moments robbing their stuff out of the bathroom, 'Just to let them know what it's like.' Thankfully though, she never got around to doing that. Didn't stop her fantasising though!

I got the class to devise Celine's exercise for her. Like Áine, Celine's exercise entailed that every time the shampoo went missing, we'd all give her a euro. A few weeks later, we all clamoured to hear what had happened.

The unusual thing about this class though, was that two of the members of the class were very close friends of Celine and knew her daughters well. Celine began her report by accusing them immediately of colluding with her daughters in sabotaging the exercise.

This time it had been three weeks since the class had met. Celine reported that even though she was ready to do the low frustration exercise, not once did the shampoo go walkies.

The teasing between Celine and her two friends went on for a while; the two friends swearing that they hadn't said anything, and Celine swearing that they must have, as the shampoo was there in the shower, day after day. After a while Celine started to accept that her two friends were telling the truth and they hadn't told her daughters.

In order to understand what had actually happened, I asked Celine to think about the few weeks prior to attempting the exercise. How many times had it happened during that time? The more she thought about it the more she realised the shampoo went missing only occasionally. So the shampoo didn't just remain in its place whilst Celine was doing the exercise.

As the class discussed how often the shampoo actually did go missing, Celine realised that instead of it happening all of the time, it actually happened only every once in a while, so she was allowing a very minor disturbance to cause quite extreme frustration. Realising this had enormous benefits for Celine. Since she now knew that it only happened infrequently, she found that she was able to accept that these things happen and that it was no big deal.

However, the shampoo was still going missing. Up to now, in order to satisfy her demand that the daughters must not take it, Celine would give out, but to no avail. Now, with the occasional nature of the incident in mind, we looked at what Celine could do to remedy the situation.

The answer was simple and provided by another person in the class. Always keep two bottles in the shower. The chances of them taking two bottles at the same time were minimal. Problem solved! And the daughters never even knew!

Trying It Yourself

So try a few Low Frustration Tolerance exercises. By doing them regularly you will find that your frustration tolerance improves significantly. You will also find you keep things in perspective more readily.

As *GROW* put it, 'We need to accept being discontent in lesser things in order to be content in greater things. So we learn to be content to be discontent in many things.'

But Low Frustration Tolerance is just one of three unhealthy emotions we all share. We will now look at the others. Note that I said that we *all* share them.

The other two emotions are: *Ego Anxiety* and *Anger*. We will be looking at Ego Anxiety later when we come to look at depression, but for now, let's just say a few things about anger.

Damning Anger

Anger doesn't need much explanation here since I don't think there's anyone reading this book that hasn't experienced it. Anger in its healthy form empowers us to change things that we find unacceptable.

There is however an unhealthy form that unfortunately we all feel from time to time which is damaging to us. In this type of anger, instead of just having a *preference* that somebody not do something, we are *demanding* they don't. We call this unhealthy anger, damning anger, 'You absolutely should not have done that and because you did it you are bad and should be punished.'

Of course if you add the caveat that 'I would like to be the one to administer the punishment' then you've hit the damning anger nail right on the head.

Damning anger is one of the unhealthy emotions that we all share. It is different from non-damning anger which is a healthy negative emotion that can help us cope with situations that we need to change.

So what is the difference between them? Basically, the difference is that with non-damning anger you are judging the crime. In damning anger you're judging the person.

Of course when you act on the damning anger you're reinforcing this irrational belief. We can delude ourselves that our damning anger is justified or tell ourselves that we don't act on our anger.

We can defend our behaviour in a million different ways, but we still do it, and it is still as damaging to our mental well-being. Acting on our anger can take various forms. It can lead to physical violence when extreme, but there are a myriad of ways of acting on damning anger that are much more subtle and just as destructive. Caustic comments to others about an individual or remarks barbed with criticism and packaged as 'constructive criticism', are some of the more subtle examples.

Who hasn't had periods in their relationships where the relationship can only be compared to a silent movie? I'm sure you can imagine the scene, 'all picture and no sound', where the atmosphere is as cold as a pharaoh's tomb.

Over time this type of 'acting out' our anger can do immense damage to relationships. However, there is a form of anger that ends up hurting nobody but ourselves, and that is the big bogeyman: resentment.

Resentment

The word resentment comes from the Latin word *resiro* which means to mull over, or to brood. And that is precisely what happens when we allow resentment to take over our lives.

If someone does you a wrong, you get angry about it, which subsides eventually and you think you've gotten over it. However like a cow chewing the cud, we start thinking about what the person has done. We bring the hurt up again in our minds and relive the injury all over again.

After we've given the hurt a good chew, we swallow it until we decide to bring it up again and like our friend the cow, give it another good chew. This goes on and on continuously and if we don't stop it, it poisons us, resulting in mental ill health or even taking revenge.

It is the continual reliving of the injury that perpetuates the hurt we feel and feeds the resentment. There is an old saying – if you act in revenge, then dig two graves. One of them will be your own.

This is very true, because unfortunately that is where acting on damning anger gets you. So the knack of dealing with resentment is to dispense with it *without* taking revenge.

I remember hearing an interview on radio where a woman was describing how she had forgiven the people who had murdered her husband. The interviewer was incredulous at this.

'But by forgiving them, are you not letting them off the hook?' he asked. 'No', she replied. 'By forgiving them, I'm letting me off the hook.'

Letting Go of Resentment

If you're experiencing resentment then the only way I know that works to eliminate it is to stop reliving the hurt. When you find yourself chewing the cud on it again and again, you've got to keep letting it go and focus on what therapists call the *eternal now*.

This means coming back to this moment in time and place and focusing on where you are and what's going on at this moment in time. By not reliving the hurt, you're not adding any fuel to the fire and over time the flames of your resentment will progressively lessen.

That's the easy part. By far the hardest challenge in relinquishing resentment is finding the *willingness* to let it go. Part of you, you will find, won't *want* to let go of the hurt. We think that if we let go then this will in some way either let them off the hook, or sell out on what we believe is right or wrong.

This is not the consequence of letting go of resentment. With 99 percent of resentments, the subject of your resentment isn't even aware, or couldn't care less *what* you think. They are sleeping soundly at night, and you're awake seething with resentment in the small hours of the morning. Feeding your resentment is like drinking poison, but expecting someone else to die.

The purpose of letting go is to remove the person and their crime from your head, so as to prevent what they did hurting you continuously. So if you are experiencing resentment, you may wish to try the following ideas.

These are by no means a definitive guide to overcoming resentment. They are just some tips that I have found useful over the years.

> 1. Be willing to let it go. If you can't find the willingness, then at least try to find the willingness to be willing. By being willing to be willing, you're acknowledging that you're sick and tired of being sick and tired. This has the effect of unlocking the door, which then makes it much easier to

open. Getting the willingness is the most crucial part of letting go.

2. Try to recognise if what's underpinning your resentment is actually hurt over what the person has done. If this is the case then you need to be able to let go of this as well.

Hurt can be both healthy and unhealthy. In its healthy form it is a warning sign that we are being treated unfairly and can galvanise us to challenge the person who is treating us this way. This hopefully will encourage them to make amends.

But what if we have no hope of getting them to backtrack on what they have done? With healthy hurt, we can let go of the situation if there is no chance of getting the resolution we want. There is a different form of hurt that can occur though. We call this *pathological hurt*.

Pathological hurt is when the hurt, instead of helping us, makes the problem even worse and in delivering a double whammy, develops a pathology of its own. Pathological hurt occurs when we demand that: *We absolutely must not be treated this way.*

Demanding that I shouldn't have been treated this way is all very well and good. But try to look at it this way. You're demanding that something *should* not have happened that already has. By the time you feel the pathological hurt, you have already been treated that way.

By demanding, you are boxing yourself into a corner whereby the only way you will be able to get a resolution is for the other person to undo the damage. This will work if they are willing to comply with your wishes. But what if they're not? What do you do then? If this is the case, you need some other way of relieving your hurt.

To do this you first need to stop demanding. This is a lot harder than you think as one of the hidden things about hurt is that if you give up the demand you can sometimes feel that this in some way validates what has been done to you, or that you have been overreacting in some way.

3. Having got this far, you are now ready to try to change your behaviour, When you find yourself 'chewing the cud' on the resentment, try to focus on where you're at today. Focus on the activity you're performing now. This will help you concentrate on your reality at this moment.

4. If the feelings start to become overwhelming then focus on the physical aspects of your reality. Sit down and close your eyes. Focus your attention on how your feet are touching the floor, your bottom is touching the seat and your back is leaning against the back of the seat.

5. Notice the physical sensations happening in your body. How your heart is beating and how the air is entering and exiting your lungs. Try to imagine what must happen in your body in order to transmit a message from your brain to your toes to make them wriggle. Try to imagine all the electrical connections between the brain and the toes.

6. Try to accept that the resentful/hurtful thoughts will be triggered. Your progress is not determined by whether the thoughts are there or not. Your progress is determined by what you do with the thoughts when they occur. If you try to demand that you must not have the thoughts

then you'll trigger them. Let the thoughts in and out, just try not to let them nest when they are in your head.

7. Take action. One of the biggest myths in mental health is the belief that emotional problems can be solved through inaction and inertia. This is just not true. It is not possible to think your way out of an emotional hole. You have to act your way out. However don't think for one minute that it's the grand actions that determine change. In practice this is not the case. It's usually the culmination of many small, seemingly innocuous ones that determine the result.

So take action! The secret is to stop living inside your own head. Instead, try to do something for someone else. This will help you to focus outwardly rather than occupy only your own mind. Or as a very good friend of mine says: 'If I want to have a miserable day, all I have to do is give myself my complete undivided attention.'

Chapter 8

Habit 2: Trying To Be In Control

In Chapter 2 we looked at Hilda's story. We saw how what was causing her panic attacks was that she was attaching danger to the actual physical symptoms of anxiety.

Attaching danger to the physical symptoms of anxiety is what we call the *cognitive dynamic* of panic attacks. That is, it is the 'thinking style' that causes the panic attack to occur.

There is however another cognitive dynamic behind this type of panic-driven anxiety. Here, although the person gets very panicky, they don't have full-blown panic attacks.

The reason why they don't have full-blown panic attacks is quite simple. During a panic attack, the person cannot identify what is causing them to panic as they don't realise that they are getting anxious about the actual physical symptoms of anxiety.

In this next variety of anxiety, however, the person most definitely *can* identify what's causing their anxiety. To illustrate this more clearly and show you what I mean, let's meet Kathy from Chapter 1 again.

Kathy's Story

Kathy was a middle-aged woman who was referred to me by her GP for help in what is usually called a health phobia. Health phobia is a quite common phenomenon that GPs see in their surgeries.

It usually starts quite innocently with the person presenting a physical complaint to the doctor and requesting that it be checked out for them. This the diligent doctor does, but when nothing shows up on tests and everything comes back as NAD (No Abnormalities Discovered) the phobia starts to show itself.

The person may have their ailment checked out numerous times and the GP may reassure the person that everything is OK but it will make no difference as the problem just won't go away.

And what makes matters worse is that the reassurance itself seems to exacerbate the situation. The person gets more and more anxious and finds themselves in this never-ending dance of wanting more and more tests, some quite invasive, as the GP tries harder and harder to persuade them that there is nothing physically wrong with them.

At this stage, the GP may suggest therapy which only serves to antagonise the patient; 'Are you suggesting that it's all in my head?' they say. When the GP tries to explain to them that getting more and more tests will not offer a solution, the person disengages, finds a new GP and starts the cycle all over again.

Kathy was lucky. She realised fairly quickly that there was something wrong with her thinking and not her body. She stuck with the same GP. Where Kathy got it wrong, though, was that she tried to solve the problem herself without realising what the real problem was.

And her answer only added fuel to the fire. Eventually, when she realised the issue had overtaken her, she agreed to her GP's suggestion that she come to see me.

Let's take Kathy's story and look closely at what was going wrong for her, because I can guarantee you that whilst you may not have a health phobia, you *do* have a lot more in common with her than you think.

Starting the Therapy

Once she was settled, I asked Kathy for an example of where she experienced the problem. Starting off with a basic example is usually a good place to start as the dynamics will be the same in the simple cases as in the more complex ones when the problem occurs.

Kathy told me that about six weeks previously she had noticed one morning that she felt slightly numb in her left arm. Her immediate reaction was that there was something sinister about the numbness.

On arriving into work, she immediately Googled the symptoms and was horrified to find that they could be indicative of multiple sclerosis or motor neuron disease.

She couldn't concentrate on her job the whole morning. Her head was in a whirl. She made an emergency appointment with the GP. Her GP was very understanding, but explained that it was highly unlikely that she had multiple sclerosis and the numbness was most likely a result of sleeping awkwardly the night before.

Kathy wasn't convinced though and insisted on a test to confirm what the doctor was telling her. Reluctantly, the doctor agreed and as Kathy told me, she waited nervously for the next two weeks afraid of what she might discover. It was when the result came back as negative that the GP finally got her to accept that this cycle of continuously having tests to prove to herself that she was OK had to stop.

As Kathy said, 'She had me over a barrel and I knew it. I

couldn't go on like this. I just couldn't face another episode like what I experienced over the previous two weeks. And so, Enda, I've ended up with you.'

Kathy continued with her story. She outlined that in every other part of her life she was a very competent person. 'I'm serious,' she said when I gave her my 'quizzical' look. 'I'm normally the one everybody comes to with their problems. I'm always told that I'm a "rock of sense". If the next-door neighbour's house went on fire, I'd be the first on the scene, water hose in one hand, phone in the other calling the fire brigade. And of course I'd be the type who'd have the plate of sandwiches ready for everybody as well. It's just this part that I can't get my head around.'

I suggested that to give us some direction, we go back to the beginning and look at what was going on in her head at the time she experienced the numbness in her arm. Hopefully by doing this, we could simplify what was going on and in doing so solutions might just become clearer.

Back to the Start

Using 'feeling numb in my arm' as a trigger, I asked Kathy how she felt when she first noticed the symptoms. She replied, 'Anxious'. I asked her what she said to herself about the 'feeling numb' sensation that contributed most to her anxiety. Kathy didn't have to think too long about this before she answered that her immediate thought was that it may be something serious.

I then put these pieces of information on my whiteboard using the model of CBT that I showed you in Chapter 2:

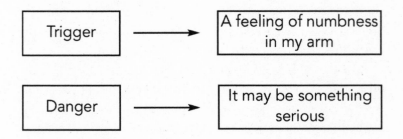

Having got this far, I asked Kathy to look very carefully at the statement, 'It may be something serious.' Which part did she feel most anxious about?

Was it a belief that there was something seriously wrong with her or the fact that there may be?

Kathy thought about it for a minute. She wasn't quite sure what I meant by the question. Surely they were both the same. So I expanded a little on what I had said.

When she first noticed the symptoms did she really feel in her heart and soul that it was serious or was it that she couldn't convince herself that it wasn't? Kathy immediately volunteered that it was the latter. That she couldn't convince herself that it wasn't serious.

'So it was the *may be* that was bothering you most?' I asked. The more Kathy thought about this the more she realised that what I was saying was true. It wasn't that she believed that there was something wrong with her, but that she couldn't convince herself that there wasn't something wrong.

We then looked at other times where she had got herself worked up over a health problem. The more she looked, the more Kathy realised that in each case what was causing the problem wasn't the actual danger, but the 'may be'.

And it was that question mark about the symptoms being dangerous rather than the symptoms themselves that was freaking her out.

Internal Consistency

I then suggested that we look even more closely at how she reacted to the *question mark* that the *may be* was causing. To do this I suggested that we look at how she was *behaviourally* reacting to her danger.

You see, by looking at her behavioural reaction we could confirm whether we had the real problem or not. In CBT we call this checking for *internal consistency*. That is, that all the parts of the puzzle match up and make sense.

Remember, all behaviour has purpose. If Kathy was really getting anxious about the *may be* then this would have to reflect in her behaviour. For example, let's say that I am anxious before giving a lecture because I'm afraid that people will think I'm inadequate and reject me.

However, whilst I'm giving the lecture, someone arrives in late. I let out a roar at them, telling them to get out and never come to my class again. This does not sound like the behaviour of someone who is anxious about what people may think of them, does it? It's more like the behaviour of someone who is angry.

In the example that I've given, there is an *internal inconsistency* between what I'm saying and what I feel. Therapists like me are always enquiring if what the person tells us and how they appear to us match up. And, do you know what? Behaviour never lies.

So with this in mind I asked Kathy to think about all the health phobias that she had over the years. When she had the thought that there may be something wrong with her, what did she do? I asked Kathy to think about this between sessions.

Behaviour Never Lies

When we met the next time we sat down and looked very

carefully at how she *behaviourally reacted* each time she felt anxious about her health. Kathy's usual reaction when she thought that something was wrong with her was to contact her GP and request an urgent appointment. Failing that, she would contact the out of hours GP service and look to see a doctor.

All well and good, but in CBT terms we still didn't have the 'smoking gun'. If Kathy believed that a lump may be cancerous then her reaction of contacting the GP would be the same regardless of whether she felt anxious about the cancer or the *may be*. So we looked at some other examples, and then we found it.

One of Kathy's pet phobias was that when she got panicky she would think that she was going to have a heart attack. She would do the usual and make an appointment with the GP. This appointment would usually be the following day, or at least a few hours following the onset of symptoms.

'So why don't you go to the local Accident and Emergency Department?' I asked. 'Surely if you believed that you were having a heart attack. Going to the hospital would be the safest thing to do.'

'Oh, if I did that then I'd be there all night. You know what A&E's are like,' Kathy replied.

As soon as she had the words out of her mouth, Kathy realised how ridiculous her comment sounded. Surely if you believed in earnest that you were having a heart attack, how long you would be kept in A&E would be the least of your worries. You'd just be grateful to be there so they could save your life.

So there we had the *internal inconsistency*. Waiting to see the GP was inconsistent with believing that the heart attack was going to kill her.

Even though Kathy thought she may be having a heart

attack, her behavioural reaction was an attempt to be reassured that it wasn't, rather than an attempt to save her life. As we now had the smoking gun, we could complete the chain of Kathy's reaction.

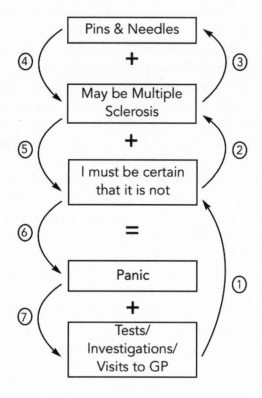

Fig. 11: Kathy's Health Phobia Chain

Maybe

Now you may think I'm being pedantic in making a clear distinction between:

1. Believing you're having a heart attack and
2. Trying to be certain that you're not.

The reality is, though, I'm not. You see, In CBT terms there is a world of difference between the two. What do I mean? Well let's look at the effect of Kathy's demand for certainty.

Look at Fig. 11 and follow the arrows in Kathy's chain, just like we did in Hilda's case starting with the behaviour. By behaving in this way (seeking reassurance etc.), Kathy was, in the short-term, satisfying the demand that she must be certain that it's not a heart attack (Arrow 1).

By satisfying the demand though, she was increasing the *may be* danger that she believed she was under in her emotional head (Arrow 2). Why? Well look at it this way. Why demand certainty about something if you know the alternative doesn't pose any threat?

The net result of this for Kathy was that in her emotional head, the *may be* was becoming less and less *maybe* and more and more *likely*.

Over time, she was becoming hyper sensitive to anything occurring in her body (Arrow 3) so that it was taking fewer and fewer physical symptoms to trigger the *may be* dangerous (Arrow 4) which in turn was triggering the demand that she must be certain that it's not dangerous (Arrow 5).

The consequence for Kathy was that, like Hilda, her anxiety was getting worse and worse with the result that she would look for more and more reassurance. However, the reassurance, instead of eradicating the anxiety, started the process all over again (Arrow 1).

Or to put it succinctly, the more certainty she strived for, the more uncertainty she found. Until *all* she could see was the uncertainty. Her emotional brain would then switch on its radar, scan her horizon and any uncertainty it found would trigger the anxiety reaction.

So there we had it. Or rather there we had what Kathy *thought* was the problem.

The Real Problem

Kathy asked the question herself. 'Why would I start doing something so daft to myself?' she mused. Why indeed. Why would a woman who was normally so in control of her life find herself in a hole like this?

To answer Kathy's question and more importantly find a solution I suggested we look a little deeper. Because Kathy's health phobia, like *all* phobias, was just a distraction from the real problem. It may have been why Kathy thought she was sitting with me, but it wasn't. And if I made the mistake of trying to 'cure' her of it then she would be back within six months with either this one retriggered or with a whole new phobia.

This was because Kathy was trying to achieve something that was impossible to achieve. The key to this is the word 'certainty'. And to understand what I mean by this, we now have to examine the whole concept of trying to be in *control*, which I have labelled as the second habit that underpins unhappiness.

Being In Control

Being in control is a concept that is hammered into us by the media every day. Advertising tells us to 'Take control of your life.' And by buying their product, we will get a little closer to being in control.

We even do it to ourselves. We believe that we must have complete control over our lives and destiny. And if you don't have this 'control' then there must be something wrong with you. But what do we mean by the term 'control' and how much control do you really think you have over your life? I asked Kathy to tell me something she had control of that morning in coming to see me. I must admit, when I asked her the question, she looked at me as if I was daft.

Kathy: 'I had complete control over coming,' she retorted.

Enda: 'OK, tell me some aspect that you had control of.'

Kathy: 'I had control over whether I came or not.'

Enda: 'Well let's say for argument's sake that you got a call from your mum to say that your dad had been taken seriously ill. Would that have affected your decision to come?'

Kathy: 'Well of course it would.'

Enda: 'So, would you accept that your decision to come was dependant on you not getting a phone call like that.'

Kathy: 'Well, if you put it like that, I suppose you're right.'

Enda: 'So, your decision to come was determined by you not getting a call from your mum. So whether you came or not this morning, wasn't really controlled by you, was it?'

Kathy: 'But I did have control over the time I got out of bed.'

Enda: 'Well did you? Did you have control over the workings of your alarm clock and the guy who made the batteries for it? They could have malfunctioned overnight?'

Kathy: 'OK, I accept what you're saying, but there are other areas of my life that I have control over'.

Enda: 'Could you name one area?'

Kathy: 'Well, my career for a start. I have control over that.'

Enda: 'And could you tell me one part of your career that you have control of?'

Kathy: 'I have control over whether I remain, change jobs, or go into work tomorrow or not.'

Enda: 'But whether you stay at it or not will be determined by a lot of factors – the economic situation; your needs; whether you are content where you are or not and loads of factors that are not under your control. Even whether you go into work tomorrow or not will be similarly determined by whether you're sick or not, or whether your boss orders you there etc.'

Kathy was getting frustrated by now. She could see that everything she was saying she had control of was really determined by other factors. So in time-honoured CBT fashion, I decided to put the boot in a bit further.

Enda: 'Even the clothes you're wearing were determined by the electricity supply board sup-plying electricity to have your washing machine and iron working a few days ago. And the fact that you arrived here today was determined by every other driver on the road driving safely so that they didn't run into you!'

Kathy: 'So what do I have control over?'

Enda: 'You tell me? Because I don't know of any-thing in life, that is within our control. We may have choices, but whether we can act on those choices will be determined by more factors than you can count.'

Kathy was willing to accept what I was saying at a certain level, but this was not because she believed it. Rather it was because she couldn't think of a good argument to contradict me.

However, regardless of how she thought about it, she knew that she was in a corner. You see, there was no example she could give me of exercising control in her life that I couldn't refute. I was able to show her that the outcome of each of her decisions was actually determined by multiple circumstances that were outside her control. If she was confused by now I was about to confuse her even more.

> Enda: 'And yet, when you made an appointment a few weeks ago, there was a high likelihood that you'd make it here this morning. So on one level I'm saying you had no control over coming, but on another level, I'm saying that it would have being highly likely that you would turn up. So what do I mean?

I think at this stage Kathy was about to give up on me. She said she was totally confused as to what I meant or where I was going with this. But in CBT terms this is *exactly* how I wanted Kathy to be. Dr Marion Dyer is a GP in Blanchardstown, Dublin and a leading figure in training GPs. She teaches trainee doctors that: 'Confusion is good, as it means that you're starting to learn something new. Learning something new will nearly always involve some level of confusion at the start.'

So now that Kathy was confused, I could show her a much more rational way of understanding what we mean by the term control. Let's see how I explained this to her.

The Explanation

The only reason that Kathy was able to exercise her decision to be with me that morning was because her world had retained enough *stability* for long enough that she had a reasonable amount of *certainty* that if she decided to attend today, she would be able to achieve that goal.

Because bad things don't happen all of the time, we are able to plan aspects of our lives. If Kathy planned or wanted something that day, there was a fairly good chance that she would be able to achieve it.

In life the more stable our world is, the more *security* we feel we have (e.g. If I go home tonight there is a high likelihood that my wife will be there, the kids will be OK, the house will not have burned down and I'll be able to sleep in my own bed tonight).

This level of security has a ripple effect throughout our lives. If my basic needs are met then I will expand my horizons and seek security in my relationships, career and so on. And if my world remains stable enough, giving me a reasonable amount of certainty and security then I will find that I can achieve a certain level of *order* in my life. That is, things go the way I want them . . . more or less.

Now look at what I've just described. Look at the four words that I've highlighted. These four words are:

- Stability
- Certainty
- Security
- Order

I'm now going to use these four words to define a more accurate description of what most people try to describe when they use the word 'control'. And I'm going to use this definition to try to illustrate where trying to be in control really gets you.

In my life, as in most people's lives, I have about 70 to 80 percent stability, certainty, security and order at any given time. This allows me to plan, predict certain outcomes and make decisions that have a reasonable chance of being achieved.

If I wake up in the morning and find that I've run out of toothpaste I can plan to go to the shop on my way home from work and buy some. However, as to whether I'm able to achieve this or not will be dependent on a near infinite number of circumstances being a certain way.

Occasionally though I will get 100 percent stability, certainty, security and order. When this happens everything goes my way. All the plans I make work out just the way I want them to. But, equally, there are times when life will pull the rug from under my feet.

Things happen that upset my plans. People get sick, economic circumstances change, relationships break up. I may even find myself reacting to things in a way that I don't like. I may mess things up, allowing all my plans to go astray. My company may go bust or I may lose my job.

During such times, I may feel that someone has driven a steam engine through my sense of stability, certainty, security and order.

However, this is the nature of life. There are good and bad times. We can try to react and cope with what life throws at us, but we usually can't control it. As a client who was from the Bahai faith said to me: 'A prince and a pauper have the same problem – a life and how to live it.'

Most of us muddle along in life making the best use of the tools we have. You may even go through periods where you get so much stability, certainty, security and order that you feel in control of your life, but don't ever delude yourself that you're in control because you're not. Your share of problems has just not arrived yet.

I Must Be In Control

Now let's look at what the person who lives by the philosophy of *I must be in control* is trying to achieve. In this case, the person is demanding that they *must* be in control.

That is they are demanding that they *must* have 100 percent stability, certainty, security and order, 100 percent of the time. See the problem? The person is demanding that everything must go their way.

They must react and overcome everything that happens in their lives all of the time. But that is just not possible. You may succeed from time to time because that's the nature of life, not because you're in control.

And what's worse is the more stability, certainty, security and order you look for, the more *instability, uncertainty, insecurity* and *disorder* you will find. Eventually, if you live your life by this philosophy, all you will find is instability, uncertainty, insecurity and disorder.

So where am I going with this? Well watch carefully whilst I 'marry' the idea of control into Kathy's health phobia. I asked Kathy to watch her behaviour over the following week.

I wanted her to pay particular attention to matters that frustrated her or when she found health issues that she couldn't leave well enough alone.

At the next session we looked at the results. Kathy noticed that when she felt frustrated over something she would do one of two things.

Firstly, she would try to change the situation. Kathy was able to give me lots of examples of where she did this during the week. She noticed that every night when the kids were in bed she would ensure that the kids' toys were cleared away before sitting down to watch TV. She also noticed that she couldn't relax unless she had everything done that was supposed to be done.

This kind of behaviour infiltrated most of what she did during the average day. If anything was imperfect in her eyes then she couldn't relax until she fixed it or made it the way she wanted it.

No Plan C

I then asked Kathy for examples of situations where she found something that she was not able to change. Kathy had to think about that one for a while. She then smiled and said that she didn't need to look any further than her husband.

She had tried in the early years of her marriage to change him and teach him to do things the way she wanted but had given up for the most part. 'Doesn't stop me trying from time to time though,' she laughed.

'So, if you come across something that you can't accept then your first reaction is to change it so as you don't feel anxious or frustrated. And if you can't change it then your next reaction is to try to avoid the situation?' I queried.

Or to put it plainly, if Kathy found something that frustrated her, then her plan A was to act and change the situation so as to achieve her stability, certainty, security and order. If however she found that she couldn't achieve this then her plan B would be to avoid the situation.

Unfortunately for Kathy however, plans A and B were the only ways she knew how to deal with things. So what would happen if she found something in her life that distressed her – something about which she could neither get 100 percent certainty nor avoid? For example, if she was anxious that she may have cancer, what would she do?

Is it possible to be 100 percent certain that you don't have some form of cancer growing in your body? No it's not. And is it possible to avoid the situation? No it's not. Neither plan A nor B will work in this case. And poor Kathy had no plan C.

The result of this was that when she had a thought in her head that a symptom could be dangerous, because she couldn't avoid the situation, she had to opt for plan A and find 100 percent certainty that it wasn't cancer. As we've seen above, this is not possible. Have a look at Fig. 3 again and follow the arrows.

Having a demand that 'I must be certain that I don't have cancer' would lead her to seek reassurance from doctors to satisfy the demand for certainty. By constantly seeking 100 percent certainty that she did not have cancer she was exacerbating her demand (Arrow 1).

Unfortunately for her, the more she tried to satisfy the demand for certainty, the more uncertain she would feel with the result and the more intense the sense of danger would become (Arrow 2).

And the greater the perceived danger, the more hypersensitive she became to the health symptoms (Arrow 3). Over time it was taking fewer and fewer health symptoms to trigger the sense of danger (Arrow 4) which would in turn trigger her demand for certainty (Arrow 5) which would cause Kathy to get more and more anxious (Arrow 6). She would then seek even more reassurance and start the process all over again (Arrow 7).

That was why Kathy was sitting with me. Throughout her life Kathy had thought that achieving the goal of being in complete control was the solution to all her problems. She never once thought that demanding to be in control was actually demanding 100 percent stability, certainty, security and order in her life. And that this demand for 100 percent certainty would be the source of her anxiety. So why was she doing it?

Just To Be OK

We now encounter another fallacy that many people believe. That is the belief that by trying to be in control, you're trying to be better than other people. The so-called 'control freak'.

Kathy wasn't acting out on the habit of control in order to be better than other people. Rarely do perfectionists aspire to perfection in order to be a perfect person and superior to everybody else.

No, Kathy, like all other perfectionists, was trying to be 100 percent in control simply to be OK and the same as everybody else. People who have this habit believe that 'in order to be just OK, I must be 100 percent perfect and do everything 100 percent perfectly.' And this as you now know is impossible to achieve all the time.

Where Control Gets You

So what's the solution to the habit? Well for starters look at what you're trying to achieve and why. If you believe that in order to be just OK you must be 100 percent perfect then you are living a philosophy that is both irrational and unachievable.

But imagine for one minute that I created a world for you where in order to be OK you didn't have to be perfect. What would it be like?

Now don't fall into what we call the *dichotomous trap*. That is, it's either black or white. The dichotomous trap is the trap where you believe that either you are all perfect or all failing.

If you are playing the dichotomous trap then for you there is no in-between. If you fail in even the slightest way then you are a failure. This is just not the case.

Giving up your perfectionism doesn't leave you at the opposite end of the spectrum. The real result is that giving up the habit of trying to be in control makes you much better at being successful in life. What do I mean? Well imagine you need cardiac surgery and you visit two surgeons.

Which One?

Surgeon A says that he is a perfectionist. That he stresses out before every operation because he demands that every operation must be 100 percent successful. And he must never lose a patient.

Every time a patient dies on his operating table he takes to his bed for a week feeling like a total failure. This means that he is constantly anxious before and during operations.

Surgeon B however is as calm as a cucumber. He says research shows that about 10 percent of patients who undergo this procedure will not survive it. He believes his results are well within that figure.

He is emphatic that he will do his utmost to be successful, but if you end up as one of the 10 percent he will not regard himself as a failure and will sleep soundly that night.

So which surgeon would you pick? I bet you would pick surgeon B. Why? You would do so because he will most likely do the best job, and won't be buckled by anxiety like surgeon A. Surgeon B is the most effective because he is not playing the control habit and trying to be perfect.

Learning How To Fail

There was once a winner of the Nobel Prize for Medicine. He was a research scientist who had invented a drug that revolutionised the treatment of ulcers in humans. At his award ceremony he was asked to what he attributed his success the most. To which he replied, 'Learning how to fail.'

What he meant by this was that nearly all research is failure. In research you come up with an idea which you try out. This most likely doesn't amount to much of a result, but even though it doesn't, you learn what you can out of the project and move on to the next one.

What our Nobel Prize winner was trying to tell us was that whilst people could see and were praising his success, they couldn't see all the failures he had to endure in order to achieve it. Using another analogy to make this point, let's look at the game of rugby.

If you are playing rugby and you get the ball, you run with it. An opposing player tackles you and you fall, thereby failing at your task of scoring. So what do you do? You pass the ball to a teammate and he runs with it until he gets tackled.

He passes the ball to a teammate and you run with the ball again. Eventually after you have failed at getting the ball over the line a number of times you get lucky and this time get it over the line and score. But you could not have scored without having failed to score a number of times first.

Now let's look at how the perfectionist plays rugby. They get the ball, run with it, and get tackled. Now they have failed to score. So what do they do? Well they can't do anything, can they? They have a demand that they must not get it wrong. So they pick up their ball and go home. You see, in order to succeed you first have got to learn how to fail.

I outlined this to Kathy and explained to her that when she attended my practice, she had the hope that I would show her how to get rid of her health phobia. She didn't want to get rid of her habit of control, she just wanted someone to take away the areas where she wasn't winning at it.

Kathy's health phobia was the one circumstance where no amount of effort would ever win her 100 percent certainty.

Now that we were at the point of looking at the solution, I told her I would be more than willing to show her how to eliminate the demand in this instance.

However if I did that and focused on solving the health phobia problem it would probably work for a while. The chances were, however, that Kathy would be back within six months with either the health phobia retriggered or else she'd come back with a whole new neurosis or phobia.

By focusing on the health phobia only we would be leaving the underlying cause untouched. And as I explained to Kathy, the health phobia was only a symptom.

The areas where she was currently winning at the control game only reinforced her phobia. Every time Kathy did something perfect or in a way that satisfied her demand, she was fanning the flames of the situation.

I explained this carefully to Kathy. It was essential that I do this because if I didn't then she wouldn't recognise the solution when I presented it to her. You see, the solution was the total opposite to what Kathy would think it to be.

The Solution

So let's look at what the solution was in Kathy's case since the solution for Kathy is the same solution for all Obsessive Compulsive Disorders regardless of their type.

Kathy like everybody else with an OCD had grown the problem by years of penny mental health actions. These actions were how she tried to deal with her anxiety so that she wouldn't be anxious.

They were the simple daily tasks that she did in order to try to achieve 100 percent stability and security in her life. And if Kathy had 'grown' the problem this way then she would have to dismantle it the same way – by doing the opposite of what she had being doing for years.

You see the knack of living is not achieved by getting 100 percent stability, certainty, security and order in your life. The knack of living is achieved by accepting the instability, uncertainty, insecurity and disorder of life *without getting anxious.*

My experience over the years has been that if you practise coping with life without gaining 100 percent control, then the better you get at it. And the better you get at it, the more your phobia looks after itself.

For some reason the phobic part just doesn't bother you as

much anymore. This is because if you focus on the problem then the problem will get bigger. If you focus on the solution however, the solution gets bigger.

So the solution for Kathy would be practising penny actions that would help her ditch the demand for 100 percent control. *Grow* has a wonderful slogan which states;

> *We need to accept being discontent in lesser things in order to be content in greater things.*
> *So we learn to be content to be discontent in many things.*

In Kathy's case she had never learned how to cope with the lesser things and that's where we needed to start – learning to cope with the minor frustrations in each day.

It's important to start with the little things. If you don't have the skills to deal with these then you won't have the tolerance to be able to cope with the greater things. I suggested to Kathy that we try out my theory with a few exercises in a bid to illustrate what I meant.

I outlined my favourite exercise that I give people as an opportunity to practise changing. Go into your kitchen and get an ordinary table knife. Now take out the butter from the fridge and stick the knife into the butter. When you withdraw it you should have a decent smear of butter left on it.

Now take the knife and stick it in the jam/marmalade, leaving a decent dollop on the knife. Next, take the buttery/jammy knife to the worktop and smearing it around a bit, stick it to the worktop. If you want to go a wee bit further, empty the crumbs from the toaster onto the butter/jam smear.

Now comes the tricky bit. Having created your messy masterpiece I want you to leave it there for *two days*.

Have you already decided not to do it? Well if you've decided not to do the exercise skip the rest of this chapter and go straight to Chapter 9 on making change. When you've finished that chapter come back to this part.

If however, you've decided to give it a go then I want you to notice how you felt when you first read about the exercise, e.g. did you feel anxious or frustrated about the *thought* of doing the exercise?

Next I want you to think about how strongly you felt about it. Mark the strength of how you felt out of 10.

1	2	3	4	5	6	7	8	9	10

No feeling   Feel strongly

So if you feel that doing the exercise would be like eating your own hair, i.e. 7 out of 10, you're ready to go to the next step.

Try the exercise. Leave the knife for two days. Now watch out how other people react to the knife. Try not to tell them what the exercise is but ask them not to touch it.

Chances are that somebody in your house will be more disturbed by the knife than you are. Furthermore these will probably be the same people who are always on your back and telling you to take a 'chill pill' or such like. (Now you have something to rub their nose in the next time they get on your back about your mental health.)

After two days, look at how you feel again. Measure it against how you felt at the start. Are you feeling worse than at the start? Or, are you feeling less disturbed? I would say that you are feeling less disturbed.

More Exercises

Once Kathy had got the hang of doing these exercises, she was now ready to raise the bar. So to instil the lesson, I outlined another exercise that you can try yourself.

I want you to make a list of things in your day that you think you have to accomplish. Now ask yourself 'Even though all these may be urgent, how many of them are actually important?' Some of them will be important and some will be both important *and* urgent.

However, it's likely that most of them will be urgent, but when you think more carefully about them, not really important.

Now take the list of the urgent but not really important ones. Take a coin and when you look at each item toss the coin. If the coin comes up heads then you may do the task, but if it comes up tails you are not allowed to do it.

The Results

So what result can you expect if you try it? You may think that it will drive you nuts, which it probably will at first, but if you keep at it then over time you will find that it takes more and more to upset you.

I remember reading one time that we only have three fears in life:

1. We won't get what we want
2. We'll lose what we have and
3. People will find us out.

By introducing the coin exercise into your life or indeed any of the CBT exercises included in CBT self-help books, you will gradually start realising at a very deep emotional level that:

1. I will still get my share of what I want regardless of whether I'm in control or not.
2) Just because I'm not in control doesn't mean that the whole world will come down around my

ears. Most of what I fear I will lose is only in my head.

3. Trying to control everything about my environment will not prevent bad things happening as it's always the curved ball that gets us.

4. People are so wrapped up in their own heads they're not thinking about me at all never mind trying to find me out.

However the greatest result you will get is what I call the *cognitive paradox*. A paradox is when two seemingly correct facts contradict each other.

Many people believe that if they give up their demand to be in control it will lead them to the opposite perspective. That is, they will lose all their motivation and end up doing nothing. This is most definitely not the case and is just an example of the dichotomous trap.

The cognitive paradox in this case is that the less control you try to exert, the more control you will feel you have. By not trying to exert control over things that are relatively unimportant, you can focus all your energy into trying to influence areas that are.

When starting out on her exercises Kathy's main fear was that if she relinquished one area of her 'control' then like a pack of cards her whole world would collapse from under her.

This most definitely was not the case when she put what I suggested into action. What Kathy actually found was what she had being searching for all these years – 'feeling *in* control without having *to* control'.

By changing her behaviour she was able to change her thinking and her attitude. As Kathy said: 'I can be OK without having to be in the Director's chair all the time.'

There is another wonderful expression in the *GROW* programme which states that: 'You cannot think your way into right action, but you can act your way into right thinking.'

Over a short period of time Kathy acted her way into right thinking. She became more and more proficient at letting go of her demand to be in control. And like many other people who changed this habit, she is able to deal with most of life's situations without getting anxious.

However it was when she saw me getting frustrated over my whiteboard marker not working and told me to take a 'chill pill' that I knew Kathy was at the point where there was very little else I could teach her.

The Red Herring

So where does 'trying to be in control' get us? Well it depends on how deeply you hold the philosophy that will determine the depth of the mental health hole you will dig for yourself.

Kathy had what's called an Obsessive Compulsive Disorder or OCD for short. OCD is a very debilitating condition to have. It occurs in people who, when they get anxious, partake in ritualistic behaviour in order to try to overcome their anxiety.

This ritualistic behaviour can take the form of certain thoughts that just keep going around and around in the persons head. It can also manifest in behaviours like habitual hand washing, touching objects, etc.

In my experience OCD is *always* as a result of the control dynamic. Stick with your philosophy of trying to be in control and you are wasting your time in trying to defeat your OCD.

Furthermore, over the years I have noticed some things about OCD that most people don't realise. Firstly, the ritualistic behaviour in OCD is never the problem. The ritualistic behaviour is how the person is trying to cope with the problem. And the problem is anxiety.

When Kathy was in therapy with me I showed her what I meant by this. If you have an OCD you can do this as well. I got Kathy to keep a note of when her health phobia was most anxiety-provoking.

You can keep a note of when your own ritualistic behaviour is more pronounced. Even though you may think that its intensity is always the same, it's usually not.

Usually you will find that there are periods where the behaviour is worse than others. The next time you notice this, look back to when you first noticed it deteriorating. What was happening at the time *just before* you noticed this change?

Nine times out of ten something happened in your life that was unstable, uncertain, insecure or disordered. It may have been an event or even just a thought.

Whatever it was, instead of focusing on the actual event or thought, your mind escapes into the obsessive thinking/ behaviour.

In my experience I have found that with OCD, the obsession is a red herring. Your obsession is the way your emotional mind is reacting to day-to-day stressors. How CBT helps is that it gives you another way of coping that is infinitely more effective.

Most of us like to think we're in control and for most of us it will do us very little harm. But for some people this is not the case. What is for most of us a fairly normal neurosis becomes a raging emotional torrent.

Toxic Stress

So how do we go from having a normal neurosis to having one that causes you to become mentally ill? Well, as I've just said above, it's all to do with the intensity of your demand to be in control. Or, to be more precise, your demand to attain 100 percent stability, certainty, security and order 100 percent of the time.

At this point you have left mental health and entered the realm of mental ill health. You're not mentally ill yet, but you are the mental health equivalent of the person who is constantly eating junk food and drinking and smoking to excess. It's only a matter of time before you develop a mental health problem.

At the very least you're living under a lot of stress that you don't need. You can observe this by looking at your frustration tolerance. Look back to Chapter 7 when we looked at doing Low Frustration Tolerance exercises. How did you do? did you try to do an exercise at all?

if for whatever reason you didn't, then let's look at the consequences of not reversing our stress. You see, as you put yourself under more stress in your life you can start developing what we call *toxic stress*.

Dr Harry Barry is a GP who works in Drogheda. He is a successful author and columnist. In his third book, *Flagging Stress – Toxic Stress and How to Avoid It*, he talks about toxic stress and how it can damage our physical and mental health. He examines why we get so stressed; and how our behavioural response to toxic stress can put us at risk of so many physical illnesses like heart disease, strokes, infection and psychological conditions like depression.

As a CBT therapist, I deal with the thinking component of toxic stress all the time. It manifests itself in people when their philosophy of being in control fails to prepare them for certain situations.

OCD is just one of the conditions that people present with where Control is the prevalent cause. However you will also find it in most anxiety disorders including severe anxiety disorders like post traumatic stress disorder. ('I must be certain that it doesn't happen again.')

Cognitive Fusion

But control, in what I believe is its most serious form, is in *anorexia nervosa*. Anorexia nervosa is a condition where the concept of trying to be in control is entrenched so deeply that it fuses into the person's entire concept of themselves.

We call this *cognitive fusion*. What this means is that the person's beliefs and concept of themselves are so fused that they cannot separate one from the other. Most people will have heard of anorexia nervosa before, however very few people understand precisely what it is and why it occurs.

Firstly, food and weight are not the problem. Obsessive food and weight control is how the person is trying to deal with the problem. The problem is that the person is using food and weight to deal with is our friend control.

In anorexia nervosa the person feels that because they can't get 100 percent perfection in their life, they are out of control. They then try to compensate by trying harder to achieve 100 percent in everything that they do and because this is not possible they fall into the dichotomous trap. I'm either all perfect or all imperfect. There is no in between. If I don't achieve 100 percent perfection in everything I do then I'm a total failure.

When the person attempts to apply this logic to their own body, they demand that they must have a totally perfect body, but of course the reality is that there is no such thing as a perfect body.

So that the more perfect they demand their body to be, the more of an imperfect body they see, until all they can see are the imperfections. This leads to a distorted image of their body; and as to what a perfect body is – hence, they make more and more extreme attempts at achieving their desired body image.

Lisa Fitzpatrick is a well-known fashion icon, television presenter and author who trained in using CBT interventions in her work. As Lisa explained to me, most of her work is in teaching women to express themselves through fashion and style.

As part of her work, Lisa has experience of anorexia nervosa first hand and it was in needing to know what to do or at least to learn what *not* to do, that led her to commence training in CBT skills.

Lisa argues that some women are trying to use fashion, not as a means of expressing themselves, but of trying to show the world that they are in control and if I'm not in control, I'm worth nothing.

As Lisa explains: 'They are doing the right thing for the wrong reason. Bette Midler once said "Give a woman the right pair of shoes and she can conquer the world."

'Well, the real secret is in learning to conquer the world, with or without shoes. And in order to do this you have got to give up trying to be in control.'

To illustrate what Lisa is saying further, I will finish this chapter with the 'AnaMia Creed'. 'AnaMia' is a code word used on websites that promote anorexia and bulimia as a lifestyle choice.

I found the following entry on one of these sites and downloaded it as a teaching tool. Even though the author has written it 'tongue in cheek', I think it captures the dynamics of anorexia nervosa in a way that no professional academic book does. Alas, it also shows the hell that the author, like all other people with eating disorders, is living in.

> I believe in control, the only force mighty enough to bring order to the chaos that is my world.
>
> I believe that I am the most vile, worthless and useless person ever to have existed on the planet and that I am totally unworthy of anyone's time and attention.
>
> I believe that other people who tell me differently are idiots. If they could see how I really am,

they would hate me almost as much as I do.

I believe in perfection and strive to achieve it. I believe in salvation through trying just a bit harder than I did yesterday.

I believe in bathroom scales as an indicator of my daily successes and failures.

I believe in hell because I sometimes think I am living in it. I believe in a wholly black and white world, the losing of weight, recrimination for sins, abnegation of the body and a life ever fasting.'

And this hell is a result of the author trying to fulfil an impossible philosophy of life that is unachievable, irrational and has got to be the most ineffective way to achieving control of your life.

Chapter 9

Making The Change

One of the most rewarding aspects of working in a career like mine has been the wonderful people I have been fortunate to meet over the years. You know the kind – people who have qualities that are so remarkable that they take your breath away.

One of these was a mentor of mine for a number of years when I was starting out. One day he introduced us to a theory at the start of class and asked us to think about it. Little did I know at the time that I would come back to his theory again and again throughout the years!

When I first heard it I immediately thought he was wrong and quickly set out to disprove his theory, thinking it would be a relatively easy thing to do. However the more I thought about what he said the more I realised that he was right.

And after all these years, not only do I think he was right, but in the simplicity of his statement, I believe he showed us a deep insight into the human psyche. So when you read his theory, try not to dismiss it out of hand.

Take some time to think about his statement. His theory was simply that:

> The only pain we encounter in life is the pain of change.

Now, just think about it. Think of a time when you

experienced emotional pain. Now think about what you were in pain about. If you look at what you were hurting about then you will realise that at the time, some form of change was occurring in your life.

This may have been having someone you love die or the breakup of a relationship. It may even have been the stress of starting a new job or moving to a new address.

However, what you will find is that in all cases in your life where you were experiencing emotional pain, you were reacting to some change that was occurring in your life.

Family therapists (also known as Systemic Therapists) have a theory which says that when people are in crises, change is occurring. Many very experienced therapists recommend that it is not a good idea to intervene when crises are taking place, as if the therapist does then they may prevent good change happening.

Changing or Adapting

In order for this chapter on making the change to make sense for you and help you make the changes necessary in your life, we need to first understand why so many people find change so difficult to cope with and why most of us avoid like the plague having to change at all.

Have a glance back to Chapter 6 if you will and check out the questionnaire that I asked you to do on measuring your mental health. In the second part we saw that:

> We change circumstances whenever possible, but
> adapt to them whenever necessary.

Now ask yourself. Which one do I try the most? Changing the circumstances or adapting? Well if you're like the rest of us, you will answer 'changing the circumstances'.

And there's nothing wrong with that. However, when

you've found that no matter how hard you tried you couldn't change the circumstances and had to adapt, how did you feel?

Naturally, adapting probably created some form of emotional pain for you. That pain may have taken the form of anger, hurt, grief, anxiety or a whole range of emotions. But regardless of what the emotion was, or how strongly you felt it, the change involved some degree of emotional pain.

So, where am I going with this and what's the relevance to making changes in *your* life? Well, you see, understanding at an emotional level that change can be painful is fundamental to practising good mental health.

This does not mean that in order to get better you've got to sign up to a long spell in purgatory. It doesn't. It just means that it's not helpful to measure your progress by whether you feel bad or not.

I find that the single most common error that people make which prevents them from implementing necessary changes in their life is the belief that: 'If I'm feeling bad, then I must be doing something wrong.'

This error in thinking can create havoc when you try to engage with a therapist. Living your life by the philosophy of 'If I'm feeling good, I'm doing well and if I'm feeling bad, then I'm doing badly' can cause all kinds of trouble when we run into difficulties which require us to change. It's also harmful to our perception of the way life and growing emotionally should be like.

So let's look at some of the most common beliefs that I regularly encounter. Following along closely behind measuring our progress by how we feel is the belief that changes can be achieved through inaction and inertia.

One of the reasons why self-help books don't work for a lot of people is that there is a common misconception amongst many that if I can understand at a logical level why

I'm having this difficulty then this will be enough to change it to something more positive.

We read a self-help book, and get an understanding into why we're feeling the way we do. This helps somewhat for a while, but because we don't put what we learn into practice the gain is limited.

After a few weeks, we find ourselves back to square one and as bad as ever we were before. So if you read anything in this book that you find helpful, then at least give it a lash.

These changes may be somewhat painful and anxiety provoking, but the aim of therapy is not to prevent you feeling bad. Rather it's to give you the skills to challenge your irrational thinking so you can change and therefore cure yourself.

However, if you do give it a try then make sure that you don't fall into the third hole. This third hole is when we try the method out and don't see the results immediately, only to give up since the approach 'mustn't be working and I'd be better off giving up on it now'.

GROW has a wonderful slogan: 'You can't think your way into right living, but you can act your way into right thinking'.

So taking action is the key to managing change. But not only do you have to take the correct action, you've got to try it for long enough to at least give it a chance of working. Paul Dalton is a well-respected management strategist. As he says, 'The good news is that this will work. The bad news is that it'll take time.'

Remember, when you go to see a Cognitive Behavioural Therapist, you're not there to *feel* better. You're there to *get* better and getting better sometimes means that you have to put up with some level of discomfort without running away.

Even though many people use extreme language in describing their problem, I try to avoid this in describing the solution. However in making this point I have to use extreme language to get it across that it is imperative that you understand what I've just described. If you don't, then therapy, self-help, etc. won't work for you.

Try not to take this as a criticism of yourself or your efforts to overcome your mental health difficulties so far. It's not. It's because you're human and because you're human you're a talented avoider like the rest of us.

And again, because we're human we all have a habit of viewing the world through a semi-frosted window. What do I mean? Well read the following paragraph out loud to yourself.

Can you raed this? Msot Poelpe can.

But msot ploepe cdnuolt blveiee that tehy can aulaclty uesdnatnrd what they are rdanieg.

The phaonmneal pweor of the hmuan mnid, aoccdrnig to rscheearch.

It dseno't mtaetr in what oerdr the ltteres in a wrod are, the olny iproamtnt tihng is that the frsit and last ltteer be in the rghit pclae.

The rset can be a taotl mses and you can sitll raed it whotuit a pboerlm.

This is bcuseae the huamn mnid deos not raed ervey lteter by istlef, but the wrod as a wlohe.

And you awlyas tghuhot slpeling was ipmorantt, ddni't you?

When we look at the world around us we do something similar to the above. We see a few pieces of information and then make a decision as to the rest of what we think we see.

When we come to a conclusion, or as we call it a *belief-based attribution*, we look for evidence around us to support our viewpoint. We then do something very interesting. Having convinced ourselves of something, we will then dismiss out of our mind any information that doesn't confirm what we believe. This is because *Belief-based attributions will dismiss disconfirming evidence.*

So if you believe that: 'If I'm feeling good, I'm doing well and if I'm feeling bad, then I'm doing badly', you will dismiss any evidence that contradicts this. It is saddening to see some people who are showing real signs of recovery disengage because they misinterpret the signs of recovery and believe that they are taking a step backwards instead.

So before we look at some other reasons why people find it hard to change, let's look at what recovery is really like. I took the liberty when I was writing this chapter of discussing what I've just written with some clients who were coming to the end of their involvement with me.

This may sound funny but in my job becoming redundant means I've been successful. When I begin with a new client I try to teach them this and how to recognise when it's time to say goodbye.

I always see it as a triumph when I see myself becoming irrelevant in their lives. As the person learns the right skills, the story behind their problem starts to sound more and more stale to them and gradually loses more and more of its potency and with that, its ability to affect them. If the therapist is any good then he should be watching for these signs and encouraging the client to disengage.

Deirdre's Story

Deirdre was one of those clients I discussed recovery with. Deirdre had come to see me with an anxiety problem that she had had for as long as she could remember. She was starting to 'fly solo' and her need for me to help her correct course was starting to get less and less.

'I knew when I came to see you at the start that my thinking was daft. I knew that it was irrational to be thinking the way I was. The problem was though, that no matter how hard I tried, I couldn't switch off my thinking in my head,' she said.

'I was terrified of everything – even little things. When the thoughts got into my mind, my head would accelerate like a racing car.

'Like, if I didn't manage to get to the gym on Saturday morning, I would obsess about it all day in my head. And this would be the same with anything that happened which upset my routine.

'I would obsess about anything that went wrong and I didn't know how to stop.

'I didn't know what normal feelings were. Anything would set me off. Thinking I might get somebody's disapproval would make me X-ray everything I did to make sure I didn't offend anybody.

'I'm sure I was driving my partner nuts with my worrying. But I couldn't switch it off. People would try to get me to see reason, but it would never work. I'd just keep playing the tape around and around in my head.

'Now however, when little things get into my head they remain . . . little things. For some reason, they don't go nuclear and take over my thinking.

'I still get anxious like everybody else. If I'm running late for a meeting I still freak out a bit, but freaking out a bit is as bad as it gets.

'I now realise that getting anxious is normal and like most other people I am much better at switching it off when it occurs.

'However, the insight that has made the real difference to me, is that my thoughts and feelings are just that . . . thoughts and feelings. I've learned how to stop accepting blindly what my mind tells me.

'And as I've done that at a gut level, I've learned how to

practise what other people take for granted. CBT has given me a whole new perspective on my life.

'I had lost so much of my life worrying that I didn't know how to live without worrying.

'My confidence in being able to cope with things that life throws at me has now grown enormously.

'I'm no longer afraid.'

Stephen's Story

Stephen was another person I talked to about the above. He was a young man who had kind of got lost in life and couldn't for the life of him figure out why.

He had done very well in school but had run into difficulties when he went to college. For some reason he found himself getting more and more anxious as his first year went on, until he eventually started avoiding going into college at all. As he said himself:

'During that first year I just found myself getting more and more anxious. I didn't realise that it was normal to get anxious when you start college. Even though I didn't realise it at the time, school had given me a lot more than just homework.

'School had given me a stability and sense of sameness for six years which gave me a lot of security that was lost when I started college. I didn't realise how having to adapt to a completely different culture, people and location could be very scary.

'As I got more and more anxious, the more and more distant I felt to the other people in my course. I was afraid that if they saw me feeling anxious, they would think I was inadequate.

'It was when I tried to fix the problem however that things really took a nosedive. I remember one day trying to face the fear and do it anyway. During that day I started to think, "If I can't do something so small as sit in class without feeling anxious, then I must really be completely abnormal as a person."

'It was then that I started to avoid going in at all. I didn't realise that to get anxious was normal and facing fear meant that it might get worse at the start'.

For Stephen, his belief that feeling anxious meant he was abnormal was a big hurdle when he tried to engage with professional help. When he realised that I would be asking him to trigger anxiety he retreated briefly.

'I had thought that you'd show me some skill where I would be able to go into college without feeling anxious. I just couldn't see the relevance of seeing a therapist and doing something that I was quite capable of doing myself. That is, go into college and feel anxious.

'I had been feeling anxious for over two years. Every time I went into college I felt anxious. I'd "white knuckle" it for a while but the only relief I'd get was when I got out of the place. Over time avoiding college became more and more frequent for me. So what was the point of going in and feeling anxious again?

'For me, learning to "normalise" anxiety has helped me face it. Learning what to do when it occurs has helped me overcome it. I've learned how to keep more balanced in my thinking. To balance the positive and negative aspects of my character and let the positive side win out more and more.

'I'm now back in college and more importantly am enjoying it. I no longer have to "white knuckle" it and am finally enjoying the college experience.'

And that's how recovery works in reality. As you work the solution you will find that the good times get better, and the bad times are easier to deal with when they occur. And the more you practise this, the better at it you become.

Growing the Solution

So how do I fix the problem? Well, you fix it in the same way that you grew it . . . by practice. There is an old saying that in order to save money you should 'save the pennies and the pounds will look after themselves.'

Well the same is true for mental health. What has made a normal neurosis that we all experience into a neurosis that is impacting hugely on your life, is not the big events in your life.

Rather it's a succession of the small penny actions that you are taking on each day that are damaging your mental health. Similarly, it is not the huge changes you make in your life that will help make things better but a series of healthy penny actions that changes the way you feel about things. But, above all, keep it simple. What do I mean? Well let's consider the following.

While it is sometimes necessary to look back on our lives to see where it all started to go wrong, in most cases we don't need to start there. Suffice to say that in order to start focusing on finding a solution just accept that you probably didn't lick the problem off a stone.

However, what has made the whole problem worse for you is that in the absence of having a compass to guide you to a solution you have ended up reacting and repeatedly reacting in the only way you knew how. It's not a matter of conscious choice that causes us to react the way we do. We just do.

In some books you will find writers and indeed some therapists arguing that you are *choosing* to be the way you are. This is complete and utter rubbish. To say that a person is choosing to disturb themselves is implying that the same person knows consciously why they are thinking and acting the way they are.

In my experience, I have found that the reverse is actually

the truth. Most of us have little or no idea why we think or behave in a certain way. We just do. And lots of people will never have to ask themselves why they do what they do.

The reason for this is because of another attribute we all share: None of us will give up our irrational philosophies or behaviours as long as there is any chance that we will make them win for us.

So as long as we're winning at our irrational philosophies, very few of us will be willing to do the work necessary to change them.

Chapter 10

The Invalidating Environment

Everybody has people in their lives that press their buttons. We all have emotional buttons that can be pressed from time to time and my buttons are no more rational or irrational than anybody else's.

So when somebody's buttons are pressed in a way that they end up needing professional help, starting the process by looking at what is actually upsetting the client sometimes isn't the best way to go.

One of the things therapists look for is how upset the person gets and when they do, how long it takes for them to self-soothe and calm their emotions back down.

To illustrate what I mean, imagine that I meet you on the street one day. And when I do I say something that really upsets you. You get angry with me. As you walk on, you probably ventilate the anger in your head and when you arrive home, have a good old rant with your partner. Over the next day or so you 'regulate' your angry emotion down.

However, let's say the following week I meet you again, and again say something that really annoys you. Up rise your emotions again, and again you use your own coping skills to calm yourself down.

In mental health terms, understanding what upset you is not the most important part. What's more important is how upset you get and how quickly you manage to bring yourself back emotionally to some kind of baseline.

We call our ability to do this our *Emotional Regulation Ability*. Mentally healthy people are able to do this very well, which, as we saw in the mental health questionnaire in Chapter 3, is why they don't get overwhelmed by their emotions.

So how do they do it? And how do we learn healthy emotional regulation skills? In an ideal world we should learn how to regulate our emotions as we grow from childhood to adulthood.

Unfortunately this does not always happen, and it was in seeking an answer to why some people don't learn these skills as they grow up that led a psychotherapist called Marsha Linehan to research why and in doing so end up developing a unique model of CBT.

Dialectic Behaviour Therapy

Around the mid-nineties Marsha Linehan was working with a group of girls who all had a condition called Borderline Personality Disorder (BPD). Linehan had come from a CBT background, however, in trying to incorporate CBT to her clients she was running into a big problem.

She found that trying to teach her clients why they were feeling the way they were and getting them to confront their irrational thinking wasn't helping.

Linehan found that when they got upset, their nervous system was reacting excessively to relatively low levels of stress. Not only that, but when they had this stressful reaction, it took them a long time to come back down when the cause of the stress was removed.

Linehan also found that by the time their nervous system relaxed something else would have invariably happened that would have caused their nervous system to react excessively again.

And it was this client group that Marsha Linehan was trying to reach out to. Nobody before her had ever found an approach that worked with Borderline Personality Disorder.

Professionals didn't understand the condition; I often suspect that it was BPD that many of the girls had who were locked into psychiatric hospitals, Magdalene laundries etc over the years.

To find a solution Linehan had to go back to the drawing board. She knew that our personality is influenced and determined by (1) our genes and (2) the social environment in which we grow up.

Linehan studied the kind of environments that these girls had grown up in. One of the things she found was that they had all come from environments with similar characteristics. She then wrote a paper in which she described the type of environment that, she said, was one of the causative factors in BPD.

When therapists like me started to look at the social part of her theory it was as if a great curtain had been opened. Linehan might have been describing the social environment that underpinned BPD. However understanding how this type of environment influences us has increased our understanding enormously of why some people don't learn how to cope with stress.

Emotional Skin

Linehan used a wonderful analogy to describe what she meant. She said that over our bodies we have skin. This skin protects the flesh underneath so that if something scratches my hand it doesn't hurt. Now imagine that all your skin was removed. Now when you're scratched, even very small things will hurt a hell of a lot.

Linehan argued that over our emotions we have *emotional skin*. This is the skin that grows as we are growing. As this skin grows it should take more and more to upset us.

However, if for some reason we don't grow this emotional skin, then even though we are growing physically, we're not growing emotional skin or to be more accurate, learning emotional regulation skills. Linehan called this the *invalidating environment*.

Now whilst this book is not about BPD, it is worth while to look at this concept more carefully. Understanding the concept of where the invalidating environment can occur in everyday life can help us enormously in appreciating why some of us can find it very difficult to cope with everyday life.

The Invalidating Environment

Linehan argued that the invalidating environment had certain characteristics that caused the problem. This is described very well by two therapists called Kiehn and Swales.

They describe the invalidating environment as one where the experiences and emotions of the growing child are disqualified or 'invalidated' by the significant people in their lives.

> The child's emotions are not accepted as an accurate indication of their true feelings and if they were accurate then they would not be a valid response to circumstances.
>
> Furthermore, the invalidating environment is characterised by placing huge emphasis on self-reliance and self-control. Any difficulties experienced by the child in these areas are not acknowledged and problem-solving is viewed as being easy, given the proper motivation.

Any failure on the part of the child therefore to problem-solve is attributed to lack of motivation or some other negative characteristic about them.

If a child is brought up in this type of environment, then they will have particular problems in trying to cope with their world. The child will never learn to accurately label and understand their emotions, nor will they learn to trust their own responses to events in their lives.

Linehan argued that they will then look to their environment for indications of how they should be feeling, and to increasingly depend on the environment to solve their problems for them.'

However, it is in the nature of such an environment that the demands they are allowed to make on others will tend to be severely restricted. The child's behaviour can then oscillate between emotional inhibition in order to be accepted and extreme emotional states in order to have her feelings acknowledged. ('An Overview of Dialectical Behaviour Therapy in the Treatment of Borderline Personality Disorder' by Barry Kiehn and Michaela Swales)

Everyday Examples

When Linehan described her invalidating environment she focused mainly on the relationship of the adult and child, where the child is the one being invalidated. There are however many different situations where this type of environment can be found.

Neither does it only happen in extremely dysfunctional families and environments. I could argue that a mild form of the invalidating environment occurs in nearly every family.

How many times have we tried to reassure our children

that there isn't really a boogieman by telling them not to be anxious? And indeed how many times do we complain to our kids when they fail an exam that they were too lazy to study?

For most families, reacting in this way doesn't do any harm and can be just enough to give your kids motivation to work a bit harder than they did yesterday. However trying to help your kids this way can have a downside.

The downside is that if doing it this way doesn't work, what do you do? Unfortunately for a lot of parents, if plan A fails they resort to plan A again. These parents don't have any other way of trying to solve the problem.

And indeed instead of plan A not just being effective, plan A creates a pathology all of its own and instead of helping to solve the problem, makes it worse. To illustrate what I mean let's take the example of Darren and his parents.

Darren's Story

Whilst I'm mainly an adult therapist, I do see children. Or rather, I usually see their parents and try and teach them how to solve the problem.

One of the most frequent problems I see in boys is anxiety. It is so common that I would suspect most pre-teen boys will experience it at some stage. It is also a problem that is very misunderstood.

For instance, in order for girls to start puberty, they start receiving huge bursts of the female hormone oestrogen as their ovaries mature.

This usually starts a few months before they have their first period. So, let's say, if a girl starts her periods sometime between thirteen and fifteen, the oestrogen rush will have started a few months previously.

In order for boys to start puberty, they start to get huge bursts of the male hormone testosterone. Unlike girls, however, these hormonal bursts don't just start a few months before, they can start a lot earlier.

Whilst puberty in the boy may not start until he reaches thirteen or fourteen, the actual bursts of testosterone can start occurring as young as eight.

What this means is that from the age of eight onwards, the young boy can suddenly experience huge emotional outbursts. These can be very confusing and frightening for him. Unfortunately, very few parents are aware that this can happen.

When these emotional outbursts occur, neither the young boy nor the parents understand what's going on. The result is that nobody thinks to explain to him why he is feeling the way he is. Unfortunately many parents don't know how to teach their children how to cope with these emotions when they occur.

These emotional outbursts can be wide ranging, but the two emotions that I find cause the most trouble are anger and anxiety. You see most parents don't realise what's going on when the anxiety occurs and they frequently make the situation worse by their reaction.

By the time Darren's parents came to see me, Darren had been experiencing increasing amounts of anxiety for about two years. He was now eleven and his parents were at their wits end as to what to do.

Prior to this, his parents described him as a perfectly normal child. His parents were perfectly normal too from what I could see, so what was causing the problem?

Looking More Closely

As I wanted to get as quickly as I could into the 'meat and two veg' of why they were with me, I asked them for an example of where the anxiety was cropping up. It's easier to look at a particular example at first.

I start by taking a preferably simple everyday example. This is because I need to look at how the problem develops in each circumstance. It's quite like watching an electrician follow an electrical circuit from switch to light to find where the break in current is.

In CBT we call this a *chaining sequence*. We look for each link in the chain to find where the problem is. The simpler the situation is, the easier it is to find each link of the chain and bring the problem into focus for the client.

I get the parents to focus on what precisely happens each time and to examine each link of the chain. It is important to do this as if you don't, the person will try to describe the problem as they see it.

However by trying to describe the problem, as they see it, they invariably fall into the hole of giving me their analysis of the problem, which is usually wrong. People will also rack their brains for a trigger that makes sense to them, but by doing this, they often overlook the actual reason.

Darren's parents thought for a while and it was his dad who gave an example. He thought it was too small to figure, but as I explained to him, it is easier to find solutions to the simple situations first.

The Football Game

Darren's dad described something that had happened a few days earlier. Darren had been playing football on the street with some of the local kids in the estate. Whilst playing, an argument broke out and during it one of the bigger lads had pushed him. Darren got very upset about this and ran into his house crying.

I asked Darren's dad to go through each step from when Darren came into the house. He told me that when Darren came into the house crying, he was watching the football on TV. He said he had sat Darren down and, using a tissue to dry Darren's tears, he comforted him. He told him that there was no need for tears and that he was sure that the bigger boy didn't hit him as hard as Darren was saying.

Gently telling Darren something like 'big boys don't cry', he also gave him a small pep talk about how you shouldn't let bullies boss you around like that and that it was important to go back out to play and stand up to the boy who pushed him.

Darren asked him what he should do if the other boy pushed him again, to which he made some 'light-hearted' comment about 'pushing him back'.

When you think about it, this is a scene that is probably played out every Saturday in every country across the world. And who could fault Dad by the way he handled it? Indeed, Darren's dad was a very loving and supportive dad who would have done anything for his son.

But let's look at the situation a bit more closely. When Darren came in to his dad first, what do you think his real problem was? Now try to think as a trainee therapist. Don't get lost in psychobabble or analysis. Keep it simple.

The dynamics that children encounter in the playground are exactly the same as the dynamics they will encounter in their adult lives. Darren will encounter as many bullies in the workplace as he will find in his childhood and the skills he learns in childhood will carry with him into his dealings with bullies in adulthood.

Therefore we have to look at what happened on that Saturday in this light. You could describe this situation as a learning experience for Darren. And as parents it was important for them to know what to do in this instance so they could teach Darren what to do.

The Problem

Let's list each of the issues Darren had that day.

> 1. Darren's first problem was that he was afraid of someone much bigger than him.
> 2. His other problem was that he didn't know how to protect himself and deal with the situation.
> 3. As would be appropriate, he looked to one of his parents for how he should 'process' what had just happened to him.

Now let's look at what his dad did. Remember too that what has happened to Darren is as severe to him as being mugged would be to an adult. The playground is a microcosm of what he will have to deal with for the rest of his life.

> 1. Darren's primary problem was that he was afraid, that by reacting the way he did, his dad was implying that being afraid in this instance was not a valid response to the situation. Darren's dad never meant for this to be the case.

> 2. Dad may have being trying to fix the problem, but by minimising Darren's tears and telling him not to cry he was creating confusion. What Darren would have picked up by Dad's attitude is: 'Dad doesn't view this as being as serious as I do.'

> 3. Unfortunately Darren will then start to doubt his own reaction and feel like it's not a valid one in response to being bullied.

> 4. Unfortunately poor Dad then digs the hole deeper for himself by insisting that Darren goes back out to play and tells him that if he is pushed, to 'push back'.

5. By adopting this approach Darren's dad has unconsciously oversimplified the difficulty Darren is facing in tackling bullies. What has been implied to Darren is that tackling bullies must be very easy.

6. Darren will then subconsciously ask himself that if tackling bullies is so easy then 'Why can't I?' Darren will then conclude that because he can't tackle the bullies like he now thinks bullies should be tackled (which should be easy), there must be something wrong with him.

What other conclusion can he come to? He doesn't see other kids being as afraid as he is. He has inadvertently learned that you shouldn't be afraid of bullies. Standing up to them should be easy. So there *must* be something wrong with him, 'because I'm afraid and don't feel able to stand up and push someone who's much bigger than me.

Compounding the Problem

Now this was just one simple instance. But let's say that the parents inadvertently react in a similar way to lots of other similar simple situations. What then? Unfortunately they end up creating a serious problem.

You see by not acknowledging and reinforcing that it's normal to be afraid of bullies, his parents were not teaching him to recognise the fear nor how to cope with it. Multiply this kind of scenario tenfold. Couple it with how the parents were reacting and can you see the problem?

As time passed Darren's anxiety was getting worse and worse. Instead of teaching him what to do, his parents were inadvertently dismissing it.

By the time I got involved Darren was experiencing

regular bouts of anxiety but had no idea what was happening to him. Neither had he any effective skills to cope with anxiety.

Over time he was doing what anybody would do in his situation. He was going to greater and greater lengths to avoid any situation that might trigger his anxiety. So much so that he had started refusing to sleep in his own room at night.

His parents felt lost as to what to do. They didn't know whether to make him sleep there or continue letting himself sleep in their room. Unfortunately they kept swaying between the two.

This had the effect of making the problem worse. As Linehan described it, by being inconsistent in their approach they were only confusing Darren more and more. He didn't know what to think or do and his avoidance behaviour became his only coping skill.

In providing the solution, my role was to teach the parents basic therapy skills so they could teach them to Darren. Considering that they were in constant contact with him every day, it made much more sense for them to learn how to teach Darren how to cope with anxiety.

This involved the parents teaching him that to get anxious was normal. How they did this was to let Darren see the parents getting anxious and translating the skills you see in this book into eleven-year-old language that he would understand.

Learning how to overcome anxiety has got to be one of the most important skills we have to learn as people. Learning how to do it at eleven is as good a time as any. Indeed, learning at eleven years of age would give Darren quite a head start at learning to be an effective adult. As the parents learned what to do, they in turn taught Darren.

Where To Find Invalidating Environments

Now you may think, interesting story, but what does Darren's story have to do with me? Well it has a lot to do with you. One of the roles of being a parent is to teach your kids how to practise good mental health and you can't do this unless you know what good mental health is first.

Above is a very basic example from a family that were no more dysfunctional than most families. Darren's parents were a loving couple who doted on their kids. There are however families that are not as loving and are more dysfunctional than others. In these families the invalidating environment can be more extreme.

In these families children are not taught how to recognise or deal with their emotions. In these families, all of the characteristics of the invalidating environment are present, perhaps to a more severe level. The inevitable result is that kids that grow up in families like these reach adulthood with very few skills in dealing with emotions.

In the example above I have focused on the adult invalidating the child. There are however other circumstances where the invalidating environment can occur.

> 1. Child invalidating the adult. In some families it is common to find children, especially teenagers, bullying their parents. When parents express concerns about the teenager's behaviour or try to challenge them about something, the teenager reacts by dismissing or ignoring any relevancy in the parent's argument. They may become violent both physically and verbally. Parents eventually start to doubt the validity of their concerns and find themselves acquiescing to their children's behaviour.

2. Abusive relationships. In adult relationships where there is a power imbalance, the abuser (which can be either male or female) will constantly dismiss or criticise anything their partner says or does that they don't agree with. Eventually the person who's being abused loses their ability to trust their own mind and becomes more and more dependent on the abuser to do their thinking and decision-making for them.

3. The workplace. Bullying in the workplace is very common. It can be from boss to employee, employee to boss or colleague to colleague. Regardless though the dynamics of the invalidating environment are always present.

The invalidating environment can be found in any situation where people's opinions, concerns and differences are not respected. In fact the invalidating environment can be found everywhere and anywhere. Even the Celtic Tiger created an invalidating environment as during this era it was common to find the belief that if you weren't 'making it' then there must be something wrong with you.

The Pathological Critic

But by far the most common place to find an invalidating environment is in your own head. Do you remember we talked about the *internal dialogue* that goes on in our heads? This is the constant conversation that goes on between our logical and emotional minds.

What if this emotional voice is the one that constantly dismisses your feelings; oversimplifying your problems and constantly criticising you for failing to problem-solve? Then it has become an invalidating environment all of its own.

People who have been subjected to the invalidating

environment eventually don't need somebody else to invalidate them. They become experts at invalidating themselves.

By the time Darren got to see me, his emotional mind was constantly flogging him and criticising him for not being like the other kids. This voice was going on consistently in his head, twenty-four hours a day, seven days a week.

This is what happens when your emotional mind becomes the invalidator. We say that it has become the *pathological critic*. That is, your mind develops into a critic that chastises you about everything.

And Darren was not unique in this. Some people who have been subjected to an invalidating environment regardless of its type will eventually end up in a world of what we call severe *emotional dysregulation*.

Their emotional skin is so thin that they find that they consistently emotionally overreact to what would otherwise be regarded as common or garden stressors. And nowhere will you find this more in evidence than in what we call Adult Children of Alcoholics or ACOA for short.

Adult Children of Alcoholics

Adult Children of Alcoholics is the title of a book by a therapist called Janet Woititz. In it she describes personality traits that people who grow up in alcoholic environments display.

Most of these characteristics are as a result of the invalidating environment. The book was originally written with only children of alcoholics in mind. However since it was first published, we have realised that the material discussed applies to other types of dysfunctional families as well.

You may not have grown up with alcoholism but if, for example, you grew up with other compulsive behaviours such as gambling, drug abuse or overeating, or you experienced chronic illness, profound religious attitudes, you were adopted, lived in foster care or potentially dysfunctional systems, you may find that you identify with the characteristics described here.

I often find that people who grew up in these types of environments often have severe difficulty in coping with their emotions, especially anxiety and panic attacks. This is usually as a result of never having been taught how to either label or cope with their emotions.

Understanding how the invalidating environment results in you 'growing the pathological critic in your head' is vital in understanding the next three habits. So let's see how it manifests itself in Habit 3: The Social Anxiety Trap.

Chapter 11

Habit 3: The Social Anxiety Trap

We now come to the habits which I believe are at the core of peoples' unhappiness. So let me introduce you to the habits of *ego anxiety* and its partner *Depression*.

In 1995, Tony Blair, the British prime minister, commissioned an economist by the name of Layard to do a study on what would be the biggest threats to the British economy in the twenty-first century.

Layard was an economist, not a health professional. So you can imagine the government's surprise when he reported that after careful examination of all the economic factors, people's health was the biggest threat to the British economy. Of course, the next question was 'What areas of ill health were the biggest threats?'

Layard found that heart disease was the leading threat. However he was also unequivocal that after heart disease, depression and anxiety were the next biggest threat to the economy. And that's how prevalent depression and anxiety are. Would you believe that over 300,000 of us will experience depression in our lifetime and that over 80 percent of us will have our GP as our only health resource? Most alarming of all is that approximately one to two people take their own lives every day and we reckon that this is an underestimate.

Now you may think that you will never suffer with one of these. Well think again because depression has a flip side where a certain type of anxiety occurs. Everyone experiences this type of anxiety and in an extreme form, it actually triggers depression.

This anxiety is called ego anxiety and it is the fourth habit that we will examine.

Ego Anxiety

Ego anxiety is an anxiety that everybody experiences. Don't believe me? Well, it's true. You see, ego anxiety is one of the three emotions we all share. When I'm teaching, I try to show this by playing a game with trainees.

I usually play it at the start of a course before people are comfortable with each other and haven't got to know me or my warped sense of humour.

The game is this. I get the class to close their eyes and sit quietly for a few moments. I then get them to visualise the most embarrassing moment of their lives. That time in their life that they would dread anybody knowing about. Getting them to keep the event in their mind, I ask them to open their eyes and look around them.

Whilst they're doing this I wind them up by saying things like 'I'm a kind of "behavioural expert" – a kind of therapist that you would find in a Hollywood film. Someone who takes one look at a person and is able to tell everything about them, solve the crime and is home for tea before six o'clock.'

Giving them my best 'beady eye', I then tell the class I want to observe their behaviour. I tell them that when I figure out who is the guiltiest looking I will point at them and whoever I point to, has to stand up and divulge to the class their embarrassing secret.

Walking around the room, I stare at each of them in turn.

Then, when they're all squirming nicely I sit down and let them off the hook by assuring them that contrary to what I said I'm not going to ask anybody to reveal their secret.

I reassure them that the point of the exercise was not to force them to share their most embarrassing secret, but to trigger an emotion. When the 'long sighs' finish, I ask the class how many of them felt anxious and as you may have guessed most of them did.

We then go on to look at why they got anxious. Now whilst I can't play that game with you, you can pretend that you were in the class and try to imagine how you would have felt.

My next question of course is then to ask, what do they think caused their anxiety? Was it me? Was it the way I stared at them? Well as you will have learned already in this book, it wasn't what was happening, but what they said to themselves about what was happening, that was causing their anxiety.

You see the purpose of the game was to trigger the emotion we call ego anxiety. And since I already knew that everybody gets it, I knew everybody in the class would have it too. I only had to find a way of triggering it – hence the game.

The Chain

As a class we then do a chaining sequence to look at what was going on in people's heads that was causing their anxiety. The chain usually goes like this:

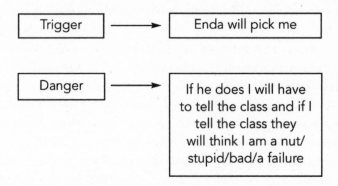

Fig. 12: Anxiety Chain

So far so good, but thinking that the class will think they're stupid is not what's causing each person's anxiety. Rather, it's what the person says to themselves about this interpretation/danger that causes their anxiety.

Or we could put it like this. What does it mean to the person if they do something which will result in people thinking they're stupid? Think about it yourself. How often do you stop yourself doing something because you're afraid of what people may think?

And indeed, how would you have felt if you had been doing the exercise? You probably believe that if people had thought you were stupid, then that would be a disaster for you. That in some way you would have to accept whatever people thought of you.

Remember that when we look at what was causing the problem in habits one and two, the *cognitive demand/belief* that was causing the anxiety was a demand that: 'It must not happen; if it does it will be awful.'

We call the anxiety that is caused by this dynamic *situational anxiety*. That is, it's the situation that is being rated as awful, whether it's the physical symptoms of anxiety or the lack of control being experienced, it is the situation that is being interpreted negatively, hence the name situational anxiety.

In this next type of anxiety, however, the cognitive/thinking dynamic is: 'It must not happen; if it does I am awful.' See the difference?

In this type of anxiety it's *me* that is being rated as awful. That's why we call this ego anxiety. Ego comes from the Greek word for 'I', and is a nice way to refer to the self in psychology when you want to sound impressive.

So now that we know that the 'awful' in this case refers to the person themselves rather than the situation, let's continue with the chain of ego anxiety.

The Chain

At this stage I get the class to look at how they reacted behaviourally during the game. Remember, the behaviour will always be a reflection of the underlying belief/evaluation.

To show them what I mean, I give them the top three safety behaviours that I find people indulging in. These usually get a laugh from the class as most of them will have done one or more of them. The three safety behaviours are.

1. Avoid making eye contact with me.

2. Some of the class will have figured out that avoiding eye contact will probably make them 'look' more guilty, so they will look at me, trying to mask their facial expression as if to say 'Well I've done nothing to be guilty about'.

3. Number 3s are the best fun though. They try to do what number 2s do, but when I 'eyeball' them back, they think 'Oh nuts, wrong call, I should

have avoided eye contact.' They then look away until they think I've passed on. Then they look at me again and when they see me still 'eyeballing' them, don't know which way to look and do a good impression of a rabbit stuck in the head-lights of a car.

4. Number 4s think they're the cleverest though and have the game sussed. They quickly figure out the odds that they may be picked regardless of whether they make or avoid eye contact. So they quickly scan over their last few years and pick a moment that wasn't too embarrassing and would be OK to share. A look of calm comes over their face and they sit there looking like they don't have a care in the world.

What have they all got in common? Well their behaviours may all have been different, but were all done for the same reason. And that reason was that unbeknownst to themselves they all acted on the same belief that: 'I must avoid having to divulge my embarrassing secret. If I do, people will think I'm stupid. People must not think I'm stupid, if they do then I will be what they think I am' Or in shorthand, 'It must not happen; if it does I am stupid.'

So there we have it. An anxiety we all share. An anxiety, though, that can cause no end of trouble when it gets triggered to excess.

A Normal Emotion

Most of us experience ego anxiety from time to time. If you go into a social environment where you don't know anybody then that bit of nervous tension that you will feel is the ego anxiety.

Most people know how to cope with it, and put it back in

its box when it occurs without it causing too much trouble for them. But boy oh boy, does it cause big trouble when it is triggered and you don't know how to put it back in its box.

To illustrate what I mean, let's look at some case histories where ego anxiety destroys lives when left unchecked. Look back at Laura's story in Chapter 1. Laura suffered from a condition called social anxiety or as it's sometimes called social phobia.

Unlike most people who come to see me however, Laura hadn't been referred to me by her doctor.

In fact, now that I think of it, I don't think Laura had ever been at her family GP. She found me on the internet after she had seen me referenced in a book. And the fact that she managed to track me down was only one of the amazing things about Laura.

For someone who had being suffering for years with social anxiety, she had never given up hoping against hope that someone would be able to help her. Her story was as tragic as any I've heard. However, even though she had been to hell and back by the time she met me, she had never given up trying.

Believe me, that girl had guts. She just kept trucking on despite waking up each morning with a gut wrenching anxiety in her gut and just getting on with it. I couldn't help but have the greatest admiration for her strength of character.

The tragic thing was, however, Laura had the complete opposite opinion of herself.

Laura's Story

Laura came from a middle-class family in Dublin. She told me that she always felt as if she wasn't quite the same as everyone else. Like they were all normal and she wasn't. She recounted that as she grew older, her belief about herself just developed. She didn't have many friends in primary school and usually kept herself on the edge of groups.

It was when she entered adolescence, however, that things really started to deteriorate for her.

'I had just started in secondary school and felt very scared. Everything was so new. All the other girls seemed just so confident and "normal". I just didn't know how to mix with them.

'I was horribly self-conscious. I felt ugly and a nerd. I used to envy the popular girls. I thought they had it all. They just seemed to be so popular. People wanted to be their friend.

'And they were just so confident and in control when I'd see them with the boys from the school around the corner. Not like me. Nobody ever wanted to be my friend. People just ignored me most of the time, and the boys acted as if they never even noticed I existed.'

Unfortunately, not everybody ignored her.

'I was just a magnet for the bullies in the class. There were two girls in particular. I still think they believed that their primary purpose in life was to convince me I was the ugliest, most stupid person in the world.

'No matter how much I tried to avoid them they would find me. No matter how much I tried to be better than I was they would still find something to criticise. And if I did things to get their approval then they used to say that I was pathetic'.

These two bullies made Laura's life hell. There's an expression that if you keep calling someone a dog, they'll eventually start to bark. Well if you keep telling someone they're stupid then they will start to believe that they are. And that's what happened to Laura.

'I believed everything they told me. If they said I was fat then I just accepted that I must be fat. If they said that I was pathetic then that was what I must be, pathetic.

'I eventually believed that I was whatever they thought I was. It never occurred to me to challenge this. I just accepted that I was a pathetic creature.

'By the time I left school I didn't need them to reinforce this. I was quite capable of doing it to myself. I hated myself. I couldn't see any good about myself. It was all bad.

'I had learned to fade into the woodwork. But I hated it. I hated that I was like this.

'I'm not the most intelligent person in the world, but feeling the way I did really prevented me from doing well in school. I would have loved to have done well enough to have been able to go to college. I knew though I would never go.

'Going to college was for normal people. I was one of life's losers. I drifted from one low-paid job to another. I would never let anyone close. Social situations were the worst. I would avoid them at all cost.

'I did try to go a few times but would stand there like a wallflower and get tongue-tied if anybody spoke to me. I could see them getting uncomfortable trying to make conversation and looking for an excuse to escape.

'And that was worse than the loneliness. Being rejected would just make me feel so much worse that I learned to never take the chance.

'I tried loads of things to try to make me feel better, but nothing ever worked. Every day was just more and more of the same struggle. It's bad enough when you can't live with someone. Trust me, it's a million times worse when you can't live with yourself.'

Laura asked me if I could cure her. I said that I didn't have the power to cure anybody but if she was willing to come see me, I could teach her how to cure herself.

The Party

We started off by taking a situation that had happened recently. This was her colleague's leaving do that she had avoided and is like the situation that I outlined in Chapter 1. I explained that I wanted to look at what was going on in her head at the time of the party and that I would do this in a very specific way.

Using the social situation as our trigger and anxiety as our emotion we started to make our chain.

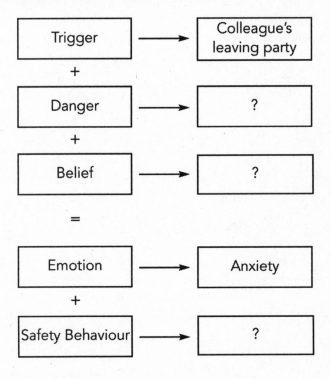

Fig. 13: Laura's Anxiety Chain

I asked Laura what it was about the party that she felt most anxious about.

Laura: 'The fact that I will have to talk to people.'

Enda: 'And what are you afraid of about, in talking to people?'

Laura: 'They will think I'm boring.'

Enda: 'And if they do think that, what does that mean to you?'

Laura: 'Well, they would think I was a boring person.'

Enda: 'And what would that mean to you, if they thought that?'

Laura had to think about that one for a while. She said that for her the thought of people thinking this would be dreadful. I then asked her what would be so dreadful about this.

Laura looked at me quizzically. 'Surely being thought of as a boring person would be totally dreadful.' she said.

'Why?' I asked. I showed her a brochure I had that was called 'The Ten Commandments for a Contented Life.' Commandment number three was, 'I promise to be boring, at least twice a week.'

'Well it's OK to be boring deliberately, but it's completely different when people see you as a boring person.'

'Oh,' I said. 'And tell me, what does a boring person look like?'

'You know,' she said.

'No I don't.' I replied. 'I don't know what a "boring person" is. Let's say I met one on the street, how would I know they were a boring person?'

Now, look at what I just said to Laura and think about it for a moment. If I asked you what a boring person looked like, what would you think? At best you would probably think that I've just slipped in a slick argument to challenge your concept of how you view yourself. But look at it again.

Do you really believe that I'm right, or does it just sound like a slick argument? Like one of those slick arguments a truculent teenager would give to a parent. You know the type of argument; looks rational on the surface, but really a bit naïve when you think about it and apply it to the real world.

However, I bet you don't really see what I'm getting at. If you're like most people, in secret you actually agree with Laura. You may not feel anxious like her but in reality you would agree that it *would* be dreadful if people thought you were boring or had some other negative trait like that.

Don't worry if you do agree. It's perfectly normal if you do, as most of us think this way. This is because the cognitive dynamic that underpins this type of anxiety is so pervasive it runs to the very depth of our emotional mind.

The Science Bit

In college, my class spent much of our time examining this whole concept of measuring ourselves against what other people think. We also looked at how entrenched in people's minds it is.

Think about it and try this exercise. Over the next few days, watch how you interact with your environment and with other people.

We all do it. We dress in a certain way not because we want to, but because we want to fit in and be accepted by people.

When giving out to our partner, do we do it in private or in public? Why in private? And if you do it in public do you keep your voice low – if so why?

A lot of what we do is either to get people's approval or to prevent getting their disapproval. Try it out for yourself. You may not have been aware that you did it, but I can guarantee that you do.

So at a surface level all Laura was doing was playing a game in her head that we all play. In her case however, instead of just acting on a common neurosis that we all share, hers had gone nuclear.

Getting people to see the error in this habit at an emotional level and it's consequence for them is one of the most difficult things to achieve in psychotherapy.

And the solution is even more difficult for people to accept and practise. The reason for this is because we all share a *belief-based attribution* that we can be measured as a person by this and that criteria, and as we've already seen: 'Belief-based attributions will dismiss disconfirming evidence.'

What this means is that having read the bit about challenging Laura's concept of a 'boring person' you will have dismissed it as irrelevant to you. You will have done this because it doesn't fit in with your own belief that we *can* be measured by what people think of us.

And if you're like the vast majority of other people, you have no interest in changing your concept of personal evaluation; you just don't want people to think badly of you.

Cognitive Fusion

In the last chapter, I introduced the concept of cognitive fusion to you. What this means is that your beliefs are so entrenched in your emotional brain they *fuse* with the rest of you, so that you can't separate the two.

The result of combining our belief that we can be rated/measured with cognitive fusion is that you have an emotional belief that is so entrenched it dictates every view you have about yourself, the people around you and the way you view the world in general.

It is also one of the biggest myths that exist in the world. One that not only do you wholeheartedly subscribe to, but one that you will to cling desperately, if I start to challenge it.

The Most Attractive Person

So why change it? And more importantly, what's in it for you if you do? Well to answer that question, here's a game for you to play. It will work better if you don't read any further until you've played it.

The purpose of the exercise is to try to illustrate to you what I'm talking about. You can do it on your own, but it's much more fun doing it on a Saturday night when you're out with a few friends.

The exercise is this. I want you to go to some kind of social situation. Now in doing this some common sense rules apply. You don't do it anywhere where you may put yourself in danger.

I want you to very discreetly 'people watch'. What you are looking for is the most attractive person in the room – the one who just seems to be a people magnet. That is, people seem to be just attracted to them.

When teaching, I try to help students get an emotional understanding of what they are actually looking at, rather than just a lot of academic knowledge. Needless to say this means they spend a lot of time playing games and doing exercises. This is one of the first exercises that I get classes to do.

Over the years I've found that the most attractive person in the room is rarely the most physically attractive person or the one with the shortest miniskirt. No. Usually the class come back with a whole variety of people, from newborn babies to the old man sitting in the corner.

I remember running a particular class where we went to the coffee shop in the National Art Gallery in Dublin. We were all sitting at different tables and it was while we were having coffee that people began to drift towards one of the trainees who had run into her elderly father and was sitting with him.

That elderly gentleman was a classic example of what I'm talking about. Without trying, he was attracting the entire class. There was something about him, that *je ne sais quoi* that just riveted everyone around him.

It was like he had invisible tentacles that reached out and enveloped people without them realising. As if he was holding court with neither them nor he even being aware of what was happening.

When trainees come back for their next class, we look at the results of their exercise. We list all the people the trainees have identified and start looking at what all the most attractive people have in common. And do you know what? Even though they will all have done the exercise in different settings, they find the most attractive people all have the same characteristics.

Trainees report that all these attractive people have a genuineness about them that is real and an acceptance of people that is authentic.

Some trainees will report on people who are able to fake these characteristics for short periods. These are people who are well able to sell themselves. They will attract others but as their warmth is only skin deep, people drift away soon enough.

With the most attractive people, other people drift in *their* direction, never away. No matter how many times you meet them, you can't prevent yourself drifting towards them.

So how do they do it? Well you could start by asking *them* how they do it. However if you do they will probably not even know why themselves. They can do something that most of us would love to be able to do, but it is in their humble nature that they don't even think about it themselves. If you would like to know how it is they do it, then read on.

The Big S

To begin to learn how to do it, we need to go back and look at Chapter 6. In that chapter we looked at Albert Ellis's Big MACS. You see, the S in Big MACS stands for *self and other downing*. Doesn't describe much now does it? However Ellis was just using the term as a shorthand way to describe something much bigger.

What he was really describing was what we have been talking about above. We call this the concept of *self-rating*. Ellis noticed that when people had ego anxiety or were depressed, they had a serious tendency to view themselves in a very negative light. That's why he coined the term as *self-downing* as opposed to just 'self-rating'.

Causal Attribution

Ellis also noticed that when people 'down' themselves regularly, they will actively look for evidence in their lives that will concur with how they view themselves. They will also dismiss any attempt by a therapist to challenge this.

As their self-esteem slips lower and lower, they develop what we call a *reverse causal attribution style*. Sounds like a psychobabble term, doesn't it? What it means is quite simple though. It all has to do with how we evaluate things we do.

Look at Fig. 14. If someone has high self-esteem and something good happens to them, they will attribute this success to themselves, e.g. if they pass an exam they will think it's because they are brilliant.

On the other hand if something bad happens to them they will attribute it to others, e.g. if they fail the exam, they will attribute their failing to bad teachers or unfair marking.

People with low self-esteem on the other hand, reverse this attribution style. If something good happens to them they will attribute it to other reasons e.g. the exam *must* have been simple if I got it. Likewise, if something bad happens to them, they will attribute it to themselves, e.g. because I failed, I am a failure.

Of course the standard way of trying to help people with depression and low self-esteem before Ellis's era was to try to get people to view themselves as having 'worth' rather than as failures. Should be quite straightforward, shouldn't it?

Well not quite. Because if you try to help people in this way, you run into issues once you start to challenge their rating of themselves. You see, as the person will actively dismiss all their good points as worthless and embrace all their bad ones; it can be very difficult to get them to stop doing this.

	Good	Bad
High Self-Esteem	ME	OTHERS
Low Self-Esteem	OTHERS	ME

Fig. 14: Causal Attribution Style

Self-Worth

So why is this? Well to understand why, take a minute out and look at what you think your own concept of worth is and what will make you worthy. Not so easy, is it? You see, the definition of worth is different for everybody.

And nobody has ever managed to get even close to coming up with a definition of what worth actually is and how to get it. So if the experts can't define it or come up with a rational way of achieving it then how in God's name do you expect the person who's depressed to get it?

Confused? Well let me tell you how I illustrate this to students. I get them to play another game. I get them to imagine that I'm an alien who's just landed on earth and wants to be human. I've heard that in order to be a 'happy' human, I need to have high self-esteem.

And in order to have high self-esteem, I must have high self-worth. I then ask the class what I need to do in order to achieve high self-worth.

Sounds like a nice easy exercise, doesn't it? The class break up into small working groups and start to discuss the solution. After about fifteen minutes we look at the feedback. And then the fun and games begin.

I first ask them to define 'worth'. Now if you look up 'worth' in a dictionary you will see that it is a measure of something. So if worth is a measure of something and you define a person as having 'worth' then there must be some kind of measuring tool.

But how do you measure worth? Can I have a kilogram of it or perhaps a metre of it? Imagine going into a shop and asking for a hundred euro worth of 'worth'.

As I ask the class to be more and more specific about how to measure the worth I'm supposed to have, the more and more lost they get. Someone eventually comes up with an idea that because we're human we have an 'intrinsic' worth. The class all give each other a knowing look and think they have cracked it.

Over the years I have often heard the term 'intrinsic self-worth' bandied around in psychotherapy. But please don't ask me to explain what it means because I haven't got a clue. And, do you know what? Neither do the class.

When I ask them to explain what they mean, the class get

bogged down further and further, using more and more vague psychobabble which makes absolutely no sense at all. Until eventually they give up and go quiet.

I then ask them to tell me what I need to do to get this indefinable 'intrinsic worth'. Now I start to have some fun with them. You see, there is absolutely no list of qualities or achievements that can be agreed will give you self-worth. You can pass as many exams as you like or climb to the top of whatever career ladder you want, but how much do you have to achieve in order to have self-worth?

What we rate ourselves and others on is completely unique to each individual. And how you will define what will give you worth will depend on a whole range of factors. It will depend on things like your upbringing, your cultural background, your own moral code, etc.

So what am I to do as an alien or indeed as an ordinary human who is depressed, if I want to have this 'self-worth' that everybody talks about? Nobody can define what it is or what I have to do to get it. I can pluck things out of the air and say they will give me worth, but if I do then my logical mind will kick in and ask how these things give me worth.

Combine this with my tendency as someone who is depressed to dismiss my achievements and embrace my failures and I have a one-way ticket to always being anxious and depressed.

And this is what Ellis was finding in his practice. In his own heart and soul he knew that he, like others, was getting nowhere in trying to either define self-worth or come up with a practical way to achieving it.

The Ladder

Getting more and more frustrated, Ellis started to look more closely at how we define worth. After about ten years of trying to define worth and how to get it, Ellis realised that the problem wasn't what you thought your position was on the worth 'ladder'; the problem was the ladder itself.

Ellis realised that for years therapists had been trying to persuade clients that rating themselves as worthless was irrational, without realising that replacing it with the concept that they *had* worth was equally irrational. And not only was it irrational, but it was also unachievable all of the time.

He realised that if you measure yourself by certain factors, then your concept of self-worth will always be dependent on succeeding at these.

So what happens if you lose at one and can't get it back, then what? Let's say you measure your self-worth/self-esteem by where you are on your career ladder. What if for no fault of your own you lose your job or are passed up for promotion? Then what?

If you can't get it back in the way that you demand, are you now excluded from ever feeling good about yourself? And does everybody who has lost a job have to become depressed? No they don't. Remember, In order to succeed you have first got to learn how to fail.

The first skill in learning how to fail is, as we saw in the last chapter, to stop trying to be in control. In order to achieve this, the second skill you've got to learn is to give up the rating game and the idea that you can be measured by whether you fail or not. And you can't give up the rating game as long as you still believe that as humans we can be measured in some shape or form by anything or everything.

Ellis spent the rest of his career trying to convince people of this. He argued that if we were to stop measuring ourselves we would be immeasurably happier.

The Most Attractive Person

Ellis, however, soon found a problem with his theory. If you get rid of the self-rating argument, then what do you replace it with? I reckon that it was at this stage that he discovered 'the most attractive person in the room'.

You see, the most attractive people the class identify during the game they play are the ones who don't play the rating game.

I don't know if these most-attractive-people consciously know what they are doing, but they seem to have an inbuilt computer chip that has taught them to accept themselves exactly as they are.

They know they have flaws. They also know that it is impossible to be perfect, but no matter what they do or don't do, no matter how much they achieve or don't achieve, they are unable to marry their flaws with how they view themselves as people. That is, they don't measure themselves, either against their own standard or against what other people may think of them.

Equally important though is the point that they have realised that if it's irrational for them to measure themselves, it's also irrational if other people try to measure them.

They have realised at a deep emotional level that they don't have to accept anybody else's opinion of them regardless of whether it's a good or bad one. They understand that other people's opinion of them is just that, their opinion. And other people's opinions are no more relevant to their lives than theirs is to others.

This means that they just accept themselves as who they are. Not only that but they have also learned to accept others exactly as *they* are. It is impossible to unconditionally accept ourselves unless we unconditionally accept others.

They don't judge others. Sure, they may get angry about other people's actions. What they don't do however is judge the person themselves. At a subconscious level they have realised that if you judge others, you end up judging yourself using the same measure. So it's not about letting others off the hook but rather letting yourself off the hook.

The consequence for them being this way is that they are generally happier than most. They have a tolerant, easy-going attitude towards themselves as well as others. In fact they score pretty highly on all the items in the questionnaire on mental health in Chapter 2. And 'pretty highly' is enough for them.

They know that they won't get 100 percent, but in order to be OK they have learned that you don't *have* to be or get 100 percent. They are also the most successful in life. They can roll with the knocks that life throws at them, pick themselves up and continue on. In fact they have a curious tendency to win Nobel Prizes!

Oh, and the reason we are attracted to them is because not only do they accept themselves, they accept us unconditionally too. As it happens, we are naturally attracted to people who accept us unconditionally, exactly as we are.

And that is why we want to be with them. They are able to view us in a way that we struggle to view ourselves. A way that we would love to be able to do, but can't as we are chained by some ridiculous idea that we can be measured by certain things, or other people's opinions.

A measurement idea that is irrational, has no foundation in reality, but is a concept so many people live their lives by. A concept that holds you back so much that you will never succeed or be happy as long as you practise it to excess.

The Raggy Doll Club

Ellis coined the term *unconditional self and other acceptance* to illustrate this but I would like to show you a much easier way to understand and practise it. I would like to invite you formally to join the 'Raggy Doll Club'.

About ten years ago I was asked to see the parents of a four-year-old little girl called Saoirse who had received horrific facial injuries in an accident when she was eleven months old. The extent of her facial injuries had necessitated serious reconstructive plastic surgery which was only partly successful.

What led the parents to see me was that Saoirse was now at an age where she was beginning to ask her parents why people were looking at her. When she would be out on the street with her mum people would go out of their way to look at her face. Some even nudging each other and manoeuvring themselves into a position where they could have a better look.

Some people can be very cruel. They didn't care how their behaviour could affect a little girl. As Saoirse was about to start school that September, the parents were very worried about how Saoirse would cope with this.

This was one time I was glad that I came from a nursing background since it had trained me into 'seeking solutions as opposed to just identifying problems.

Ideology is the luxury of those who don't have to find a solution to the mess. What could we do to help Saoirse? It's hard enough to get the concept of unconditional self-acceptance across to an adult. How on earth do you teach it to a four-year-old?

It was whilst trying to think of a way that I remembered a television cartoon that used be on UTV during the eighties called *The Raggy Dolls*.

The Raggy Dolls was set in Grime's toy factory. When a toy came off the conveyor belt that was broken or had something wrong with it, a big hand removed it and threw it in the reject bin. *The Raggy Dolls* were the adventures of all the toys in the reject bin.

All the characters had something wrong with them. There was Princess who had been stuffed with rags instead of foam due to funding difficulties. Claude, who had fallen out of the French toy lorry. Sad Sack, who was too big to be mass-produced. Dotty, who had paint spilt all over her. Hi-Fi who had problems with his inner wiring and Lucy who had been sewn with faulty tread so her limbs kept falling off.

The philosophy that the creator of the programme was trying to get across to children was encapsulated in the storylines. Read the words of the title music and you'll get the idea.

> It's not much of a life when you're just a pretty face.
> Just to be whoever you are is no disgrace.
> Don't be scared if you don't fit in,
> Look who's in the reject bin.
> It's the Raggy Dolls, Raggy Dolls,
> Dolls like you and me.
> Raggy Dolls, Raggy Dolls,
> Made imperfectly.
>
> So if you've got a bump on your nose,
> or a lump on your toes
> Do not despair – Be like the Raggy Dolls and say
> I just don't care.
>
> Coz, Raggy Dolls, Raggy Dolls are happy just to be.
> Raggy Dolls, Raggy Dolls, dolls like you and me.'

Contacting UTV, I managed to get some videos of the series (these were the days before You Tube), and the parents started showing them to Saoirse. We then slowly taught her how to start living her life according to the lyrics.

When I started running courses in low intensity CBT for health professionals I found that most of them found it very hard to grasp the concept of *unconditional self-acceptance*.

When I explained it in terms of *The Raggy Dolls* however,

they grasped it at an emotional level much easier. In fact they loved the concept – hence the formation of the 'Raggy Doll Club'.

So if 'you're not at ease with your knobbly knees or your fingers are all thumbs' then 'stand on your two left feet and join your raggy doll chums'. Joining is quite easy. You're a member when you want to be, and you cancel your membership when you decide to.

There are only four rules for membership:

1. You admit that you're not perfect, that you never were, nor will you ever be. (But neither is anybody else).

2. You've screwed up in a big way at least once in your life. (But so have most people. And for those that haven't, it's only a matter of time before they do, since it's not possible to go through life without screwing up sometimes.)

3. You can't be measured by your screw-ups as there is no measuring tool.

4. You don't have to accept anybody else's opinion of you, as their opinion of you is no more valid than your opinion of them.

Of course, if you want to cancel your membership, then all you have to do is start measuring yourself again or accepting other people's opinion of you.

So, hands up anybody who thinks they're *not* entitled to membership? I ask this to every class and every person I teach, and do you know what, after all these years I'm still waiting for someone to raise their hand. This is because we all kind of know that we're not perfect.

The Dichotomous Trap

That doesn't stop some people trying to be perfect though. When I initially introduce the idea of unconditional self-acceptance to them I get some serious challenges from students to what they *think* I mean.

You would think that the concept of the Raggy Doll Club would be a fairly straightforward idea for people to grasp. Think again. When I introduce it to classes I see trainees rolling up their sleeves to take me on.

Whilst most people can agree to some extent about what I'm talking about, their conceptualisation of the Raggy Doll Club is more akin to a fluffy puppy than a serious psychological theory. For them the idea of a Raggy Doll Club is a wonderful ideal, like world peace and Ireland winning the world cup, but not a very practical or realistic concept.

This is because most people think that the idea of rating ourselves is actually a positive thing. They believe that it actually makes us strive for higher goals and if we didn't indulge in rating ourselves it would mean less than perfect standards and therefore accepting mediocrity. You might think that yourself. But when you think about it, can you see the flaw in the 'rating' argument?

Well for starters, if you do think this way you are falling into the *dichotomous trap*. Or to put the term in plain speak, you think that if you're not at one extreme then you are automatically at the other extreme. In this case, the dichotomous trap means that if you give up your rating and perfectionist demands, this will lead you to a life of mediocrity and failure.

Of course if you do hold this dichotomous belief, it will lead you to dismiss any theory that contradicts this. (Remember, 'belief-based attributions will dismiss disconfirming evidence'.) However, even though people think they are so right, they couldn't be more wrong.

Playing the rating game is guaranteed to prevent you

winning at this game of life. It causes so much misery that it prevents you from ever reaching your full potential. It is also the main 'thinking' error in depression. In fact it's the main problem in depression.

The Pathological Critic

So how does a common or garden anxiety that everybody has create so many problems for so many people? And why does it create these problems for *some* people and not for others?

The simple answer is that like the other habits, it depends on how fixed you are in your belief. Some people play the rating game to themselves, but when they find they are not winning at it, they are able to use their logical mind to correct their thinking. When faced with failure or people's disapproval, they are able to look logically at their situation in real time. They are then able see the irrationality of their rating and are able to ditch it in the short term.

However, as they continue on in life they start winning at a few things (it's impossible to fail at everything), convince themselves that they have some kind of intrinsic worth, and go back to their old irrational ways like the rest of us. I can't say that it makes them any happier, but at least they are able to function on a daily basis.

Not so for others. For people who develop problems with this type of anxiety and depression, they are not able to switch it off.

In Dr Harry Barry's book *Flagging the Problem*, he describes why this happens:

> • We all have a logical and an emotional brain which are in constant communication with each other. Generally, although the emotional brain is stronger the logical brain is able to overrule it if necessary.

• So if we find ourselves becoming too anxious or depressed, our logical brain moves in to calm things down.

• For some people however, due to a combination of genes and upbringing this ability of the logical brain to switch off the emotional becomes weakened and the logical brain becomes swamped by the negative barrage emanating from the latter.

• This leads to the cognitive and physical symptoms of anxiety and depression.

What this means in *thinking* terms is that the emotional mind is constantly talking to the person. This one-way conversation is always the same. It's always negative, critical and judgemental. So what do our emotional minds say when we're feeling ego anxiety and depression? And why does it do it?

In Chapter 7 we looked at invalidating environments. Read it over again for yourself before you continue on. As I said in that chapter, the most common place to find the invalidating environment is in our *own emotional mind*. In Laura's case, her emotional mind had developed into what we call her pathological critic.

I think the term pathological critic speaks for itself. You see, Laura didn't need someone else to criticise her. She was very capable of doing it to herself. All the messages firing from her emotional mind were her critic being merciless on her.

Can you imagine a teacher/boss/parent or someone whom you think is so accurate that their opinion is automatically right, standing beside you 24/7 constantly finding things to criticise you about? Well this is what was happening in poor Laura's head. And indeed this is the same dynamic that happens in the head of everybody who gets depressed and anxious.

To make matters worse Laura was accepting blindly what the critic was saying without ever questioning its accuracy. She was combining this with what all the bullies she had met over the years had tried to convince her of. Taking these ingredients she would make a 'cake' of self-criticism where everything was mixed up into one big jumble. Having convinced herself of her conclusions, she would then act in a way that would reinforce this.

Having completed the 'cake' she would believe that this evaluation of herself would be what everybody else would think if she didn't go to extreme lengths to prevent it. Dismissing any evidence that might contradict her opinion of herself, she was now in an emotional hole that she had no hope of getting out of herself.

We have discussed cognitive fusion before. Well nowhere else will you find it in greater depth than in *social anxiety*. Laura's self-criticism and rating was so entrenched that her whole body and mind were locked in trying to protect herself, which was leaving her no room to do much else.

The Trial

The classic book *The Trial*, written by the famous German-speaking author from Prague, Franz Kafka, is about a man who finds himself in an imaginary courthouse where he is constantly on trial. All the prosecutors, judge and jury are denigrating him for being such an evil person.

The problem is however, that even though they are all criticising him, nobody will tell our hero precisely what he is supposed to have done wrong. All the criticisms are totally vague; there is no substance to them. No matter how he tries to find out what he has done wrong, nobody will tell him his crime. Everybody in the courthouse however 'knows' that he is in some way bad and evil.

In the Irish language there is an expression: *Dúirt bean liom go ndúirt bean léi*, that is, 'He said this that you said that.'

This is what is happening in your emotional brain. It is constantly chattering to you, acting out all the roles of the people in the courtroom.

Look at the word 'vague' again. This is where the pathological critic gets all its power from. You see, in being exceptionally vague in its criticism, Laura couldn't fight against it.

Trying to fight a vague criticism is like trying to box your shadow. You have no target on which to land a punch. What can you argue against that you're not, when you don't even know what it is you're supposed to be?

This means that *you can never win*. Why? Well let's look at why it's nearly impossible to fight against it. You get a thought in your head that you're a gobshite, an idiot, or a nerd because you did something or someone criticised you.

You manage to argue that maybe you are not a complete and utter gobshite. However just as you start to win your battle, your 'pathological critic' changes the goalposts and accuses you of being a gobshite over something else.

And so on and on it goes. No matter how hard you try you can never win against your critic. It remains vague in the extreme, constantly changing the goalposts. Over time you end up in a never-ending chase around the mulberry bush trying to catch a judgmental 'will-o'-the-wisp' that keeps disappearing and reappearing.

However, whilst the pathological critic's strength is in its vagueness; this vagueness is also its major weakness. Because if you can learn how to challenge it and pin it into a corner, you, can beat it.

Beating the Critic

How you beat the pathological critic is to take each criticism individually. Look at what the critic is saying and challenge it to be more precise. Demand your critic to tell you exactly what it is you are supposed to have done wrong.

Usually this is as far as you will get. Precision won't come easily to your critic. However on the few occasions that it can be, challenge it to provide some evidencefor its judgement. The more you challenge it, the less and less rational your critic will sound.

That was why I asked Laura to tell me what a boring person looked like. What I was really doing was challenging her pathological critic. Laura may have believed what it was telling her, but I sure as hell wasn't. By believing the vague term 'boring person', Laura had a vague idea in her head that there was a type of person out there that would fit a formula of what a boring person was. I had just got into the ring with her pathological critic.

And that was why she was stumped. All her life Laura had accepted at face value what her pathological critic was telling her. With my help, she was going to learn how to stop accepting this blindly. If Laura wanted me to accept her criticism of herself, she would have to give me some logical evidence to support it.

And that's how CBT works. As therapists, we teach the person how to challenge what their emotional mind is telling them. All the rubbish that Laura had blindly believed about herself was going to be challenged item by item, piece by piece. In each session we looked at how she was viewing the world, what she thought this meant for her and most importantly how she was reacting in her behaviour.

Common Thoughts

A lot of people think that the feelings and thoughts that they have are unique to them. Not so. Over the years many professionals have noticed that people who are anxious in social situations tend to have the same thoughts and act in the same ways.

As such, it wasn't long before we started to draw up lists of the most common thoughts and behaviours. There are loads of them to be found on the internet. Just put 'Social Cognitions Questionnaire' and 'Social Behaviour Questionnaire' into any search engine and you will find them. I have replicated below the two I've been using for years.

They were devised by Adrian Wells, Lucia Stopa and David Clarke in 1993. If you do experience a lot of anxiety in social situations, look at the list of thoughts below. Note how many of them you experience the next time you are in a social situation.

Look at each thought below and mark on the left, from 1 to 5, how often you have the thought, according to whether the:

1. Thought never occurs
2. Thought rarely occurs
3. Thought occurs half the time when I'm anxious
4. Thought usually occurs.
5. Thought always occurs when I'm anxious.

1) I will be unable to speak.

2) I am unlikeable.

3) I am going to tremble or shake uncontrollably.

4) People will stare at me.

5) I am foolish.

6) People will reject me.

7) I will be paralysed with fear.

8) I will drop or spill things.

9) I am going to be sick.

10) I am inadequate.

11) I will babble or talk funny.

12) I am inferior.

13) I will be unable to concentrate.

14) I will be unable to write properly.

15) People are not interested in me.

16) People won't like me.

17) I am vulnerable.

18) I will perspire.

19) I am going red.

20) I am weird/different.

21) People will see I'm nervous.

22) People will think I'm boring.

Now having done that, look at each answer, especially the ones where you have marked 3, 4 or 5.

Ask yourself how much you believe each thought to be true:

---

0 percent. . . . . .100 percent

I don't believe
the thought to
be true

I am completely
convinced this
thought is true

You will probably be surprised to find is that each time you get anxious you nearly always have the same thoughts. As to how much you accept them to be true however, will usually be determined by your subsequent behaviour.

Common Behaviours

So now let's turn our attention to your behaviour when you feel anxious. Listed below are the top twenty-seven safety behaviours that people indulge in when they feel anxious. Mark them according to whether you:

1. never do it
2. sometimes do it.
3. often do it
4. always do it

1) Use alcohol to manage anxiety.

2) Try not to attract attention.

3) Make an effort to get your words right.

4) Check that you're coming across well.

5) Avoid eye contact.

6) Talk less.

7) Avoid asking questions.

8) Try to picture how you appear to others.

9) Grip cups or glasses tightly.

10) Position yourself so as not to be noticed.

11) Try to control shaking.

12) Choose clothes that will prevent or conceal sweating.

13) Wear clothes or makeup to hide blushing.

14) Rehearse sentences in your mind.

15) Censor what you are going to say.

16) Blank out or switch off mentally.

17) Avoid talking about yourself.

18) Keep still.

19) Ask lots of questions.

20) Think positively.

21) Stay on the edge of groups.

22) Avoid pauses in speech.

23) Hide your face.

24) Try not to think about other things.

25) Talk more.

26) Try to act normal.

27) Try to keep a tight control of your behaviour.

Now look at your two lists and compare the results over a few weeks whenever you go into a social situation. It's highly probable that you will find the same pattern happening over and over again. And you always thought you were unique in feeling like this, didn't you? That everybody else was normal except you. Not so. You're actually the same as the rest of us. The only problem is that you've just accepted some things that are simply not true.

Solving the Problem

Of course, finding the problem is only the first stage. Now we have to solve it. So keep it simple and try this exercise as a starting point. Choose one of the more innocuous behaviours like gripping cups tightly. Now when you go into a social environment try not to indulge in this particular behaviour.

Your anxiety will probably be more noticeable. Try not to attach any relevance to this. You're just having what we call a *hot cognition* and all you're doing is triggering voluntarily what you usually avoid. Now when you're feeling anxious try to identify what you are feeling anxious about.

Which of the top twenty-two thoughts do you believe? If you can identify which one, then keep a short note of it. If your own particular thought isn't on the list, then keep a note of it too.

When you've finished, take the results of your experiment and identify one of the more common thoughts that you've experienced, like 'I am weird/different'.

Now ask yourself what it is that you are basing your belief on. In other words, what evidence have you got to support your argument? Try to be quite strict in this. Your emotional mind will try to get all woolly and vague but actively challenge it to give you some proof that your belief is true.

Most of the time, you won't be able to come up with any substantive proof. This is because your anxiety has its strength in its vagueness. When you try to get it to be very specific, it can't. As you go through the 'evidence', try to look at it using your logical mind. Does what your emotional mind is saying sound logical? Does it really sound logical that if you believe someone thinks you are weird that they are actually thinking that?

Or if you have irrefutable evidence that someone *does*, then where is it written down that you have to accept their opinion. As I sometimes ask: 'How many people must think you're a duck in order for you to accept that you're a duck?' Sound daft? Well it's no dafter than thinking that you can be rated as a failure if somebody else thinks you are.

Chapter 12

Habit 4: The Depression Pathway

In the last chapter I used Laura's story to introduce the concept of Ego/Social Anxiety. Laura had what's called social anxiety. The reason I used social anxiety to illustrate how ego anxiety manifests, is that in social anxiety the habit of ego anxiety is probably at its strongest. However, ego anxiety crops up in a myriad of other places that are usually not as readily noticeable.

Remember, ego anxiety is an emotion that *all* of us have. You may think that you don't have it and that you are so confident in yourself that you don't care what other people think of you. The reality is, however, that if you don't experience anxiety about how other people view you, it's probably only because at the moment you aren't at risk of feeling people's disapproval, that's all.

At the moment, you are winning at the 'rating game' and satisfying your own irrational demands. We all do it. You may not be fully aware all the time that you are, but this is just because at the moment you are winning or at least not losing too much.

The concept of rating is so prevalent in society that it is well-nigh impossible to avoid it. And if you don't agree with me then perhaps you can explain why sales of 'high-quality' toilet paper increase dramatically during the Christmas season.

However, let's say you are one of the few people who really couldn't give a toss what people think of you (and of course buy Lidl's toilet paper), don't think you're out of the woods because you're not.

Ego anxiety has another sting in its tail. You see, ego anxiety isn't triggered by the possibility of hearing others' negative rating of us alone. It's also triggered when we're in danger of giving a negative rating to ourselves. What do I mean? Well as we saw, social anxiety is when we are afraid that other people will speak badly of us.

Ego anxiety in its other form is triggered when we start rating ourselves based on not achieving what it is *we rate ourselves on*. To elaborate, let's meet Helen.

Helen's Story

Helen was a client who found herself in the ego anxiety hole. She had experienced bouts of depression for years. She would have periods where she was not depressed, but she could never manage to shake it off completely.

By the time she arrived with me she had had a number of admissions to hospital but despite all her efforts she always found herself just waiting for the next one.

When we met for the first time, Helen kicked off by saying that she didn't really think she should be in therapy since at the moment she was not feeling depressed. She volunteered that it had been some months since she had had a bout of depression and surely she should be waiting until this happened before engaging with me.

I assured her that whilst she was feeling OK at the moment, this was probably the best time to engage as it would give us an opportunity to look at what was happening to her that was repeatedly causing her to become depressed.

I then asked Helen to briefly look back to the previous time when she became depressed. More importantly I wanted her to focus on the time immediately *before* she noticed herself getting depressed. Helen felt a bit lost about this. She definitely knew when she was getting depressed, but never really thought about what went on between bouts; only that she didn't feel depressed. Therefore to help her, I asked her a very simple question:

'When you're not depressed do you ever feel anxious?'

'Oh yes,' she replied. 'I am always anxious.'

When I asked her to elaborate, she explained that even though she would describe herself as feeling OK, this would not mean that she was feeling happy. Rather it was that she was just not feeling depressed.

Having explained that even though she didn't feel depressed, she did feel anxious, we looked at this anxiety and I asked her for an example of when she felt anxious in the last couple of weeks.

Helen thought for a moment. She then gave the example from the previous month when she returned to work after being out sick and felt anxious about it. We drew a chaining sequence in order to look at what was causing her anxiety. Her thinking chain went something like this:

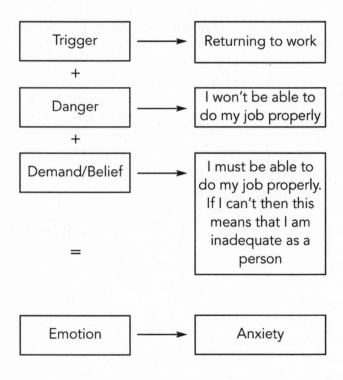

Fig. 15: Helen's Anxiety Chain

We then looked at her underlying belief that she would be inadequate if she wasn't able to do her job properly. What was she basing this on? Helen argued that surely if she wasn't able to do what other people were able to do then this would mean that she was inadequate as a person.

I asked her was this the only thing that she would rate herself on. Helen thought about this for a while. Like most people, Helen hadn't really thought about it in depth before. Most of the time, she just accepted whatever her mind was saying to her. I explained that from now I wanted her to stop just accepting what her mind was telling her without question and start looking at it more carefully.

This Helen did as a homework exercise between sessions. When she returned a few weeks later we looked at how she got on. Helen started by saying that what had surprised her at first was how often she got anxious.

Before coming to see me, she had always just accepted the anxiety as part of her depression. I had explained to her that whilst her anxiety was related to her depression, in 'thinking' terms there was a distinct difference between the two.

The variety of things that made her anxious was a new realisation for Helen. Helen had realised that she was living her life anxious if anything should go wrong or if she might make a mistake. As if she did she would flog herself mercilessly.

Helen said that she had always been very hard on herself. She would be very critical if she didn't achieve what she thought she should be able to do. Over the subsequent sessions we built on this understanding.

We examined each time she was brutal with herself, how she was demanding certain things of herself and how she viewed herself as a complete failure if she failed just once.

As soon as Helen understood this, it was fairly easy for her to understand that her bouts of depression were caused by these instances when she didn't measure up to one of her demands. Helen believed that if she failed at one of her demands, this meant that she was a now a failure in general. And it is this conclusion that one is a failure that is the 'thinking' dynamic of depression.

Measuring Ourselves

You can identify your 'measurement' of yourself by doing this simple exercise. Take a good look at what it is you rate yourself on. It may be on how well you do in your career, your relationships, how perfectly you rear your children or how successful they turn out to be. Now imagine how you would feel if you started failing at any of these pursuits.

Typically you will start feeling anxious about it. The anxiety will not manifest itself as a panicky type of anxiety. Rather it will feel more like a sick, low-grade 'churning' in your stomach. This is the ego anxiety.

Now imagine that, however hard you tried, you kept failing at your measurement. If this happened then instead of you being afraid that you *will* be a failure if you fail, you now convince yourself that you *are*. This is when you start to become depressed.

When I'm training therapists, I throw out a 'casual' comment at the start of the course. I tell them that the only reason that they are sitting in the therapist's chair and the client is sitting in the client's chair is because at the moment the therapist is winning at their own bullshit.

If you can accept that we all play the rating game, then you have come a long way to understanding the whole concept of depression, why so many of us become depressed and why depression has been identified as the second biggest health threat in the world today.

The Pathway

So, having grasped the concept of the rating game, I would like to introduce you to habit four and what I term *The Depression Pathway*. The reason that I've bunched the two of them together is because ego anxiety is directly related to depression. What do I mean? Well let's look at the following pathway. Look at Fig. 17, and follow the arrowed pathway 'A'.

Start with the idea that we all play the rating game to some degree. Now think of when, instead of being flexible with your demands, you demand that certain things *absolutely* must not be the way they are because if they are then it will mean you are a failure. For example I must not fail an exam, if I do then I will be a failure. This is arrow 'A'.

Initially you will be highly anxious because the exam, instead of being a means towards an end as it should be, becomes a measurement of you as a person. You don't regard yourself as a failure yet, but you will be if you fail the exam.

Now think what will happen if you then fail the exam or don't achieve your demand. If this happens then you will regard yourself as a failure. This is arrow 'B'. In the ego anxiety part, you will only be a failure if you fail.

Now having failed you start to follow arrow 'B'. That is, you start accepting that this means you must be a failure (arrow 'C').

This is when you will become depressed or, as Dr Harry Barry describes in his book *Flagging the Therapy*, experience 'depression with a little "d". No real problem yet. You rationalise that you can get your good rating back if you pass the *next* time.' The result of this, maybe, is that you try that bit harder at the next exam attempt.

However, since you're still doing the exam for the wrong reason (i.e. to be OK as a person) then you will go back to being ego anxious (arrow 'D') and you find yourself demanding once again that you *must* pass it this time (arrow 'A' again).

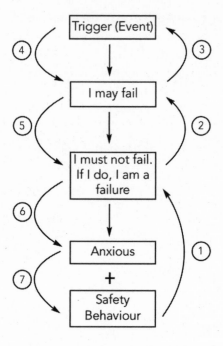

Fig. 16: Ego Anxiety Pathway

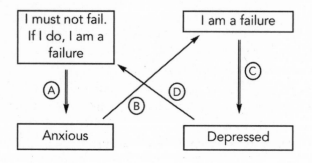

Fig. 17: The Depression Pathway

Repeating the Pathway

If however, you fail *again*, you are heading for trouble. Failing the exam will result in you reinforcing that you must be a failure because you keep failing the exam.

However, even though you may have it, at no stage is the ego anxiety/depression actually helping you get the exam. In fact it's actually making getting the exam a lot harder since instead of having one difficulty (passing the exam), you have two (I will be/am a failure if I fail).

Over time, you will find that trying to pass the exam gets harder and harder. This is because your second difficulty (I will be/am a failure) starts overshadowing the first (the exam).

Eventually your ego anxiety/depression pathway starts to develop a life of its own. You stop focusing on trying to get the exam and instead keep focusing on how big a failure you are and trying to save yourself from being one.

And once this happens, you start looking at other things going on in your life. Unfortunately, the more you try to see your successes the more you see your failures. Eventually you end up in a world where you are unable to see anything but what you are failing at.

This becomes so entrenched as time passes that the actual structure and chemistry of your brain starts to change. Your emotional brain develops into the 'pathological critic' and starts firing 'failure' signals that your logical brain can't switch off. (Remember, 'belief-based attributions will dismiss disconfirming evidence'.)

This results in a cascade of 'failure' thoughts pouring from your emotional brain that you are unable to prevent. Like Laura and Deirdre in previous chapters, your attempts are futile and you just can't see the opposite of what you're thinking or how irrational you are being.

Your pathological critic gets stronger and stronger and

your logical mind gets weaker and weaker until all you can see is that you are a failure. This is when you start exhibiting all the hallmarks of major depression or as Harry Barry calls it, 'Depression with a big "D".

Applying It To Yourself

Look at Fig. 17 again, and apply it to whatever you rate yourself on. Follow the arrows beginning with Letter 'A'. This is the first step. As you stop satisfying your demands you start to believe that you are a failure.

You are now at the anxious stage. As you get more anxious you travel along arrow 'B', that is, instead of only being a failure if you fail, you now start to believe you *are* a failure (arrow 'C').

You have now become depressed. The *cognitive dynamic* of depression is 'I am a failure'. In the early months/years of playing this game you will try to dispute this with yourself and indeed if you seek some professional help, they will probably try to convince you as well that you are not a failure.

However, even though you have convinced yourself that you're *not* a failure, by not challenging the ego anxiety part, you will still believe that you will be a failure if you fail again. The result of this will be that you will go back to the anxiety stage, arrow 'D' and start demanding all over again that you don't fail etc (arrow 'A')

As it is impossible to never fail at anything, this is an unachievable demand. Therefore it is only a matter of time before you fail again, convincing yourself that you are a failure and starting the cycle all over again.

Eventually you stay at the depressed stage. You despairingly give in. No matter how hard you try, you can't beat it. What's the point? It doesn't matter what you do, you keep failing to satisfy your own demands.

By the time you have reached this stage you are in need of professional help. It's very unlikely that you will be able to dig your way out of the hole without help. Your thinking dynamics have become so convoluted in your mind that they are like a fishing line that has become tangled.

Half of the time you will be convincing yourself you're a failure without even knowing which particular 'failure' you're basing it on this time. I described the pathological critic in the last chapter. Well the longer you remain in the 'Depression pathway', the stronger it becomes.

The Pathological Critic

I talked about Franz Kafka's book *The Trial* in the last chapter. Well this is precisely what your pathological critic does. It is the merciless voice in your emotional head that presents these vague criticisms about you and about what a failure you are. It is the voice of the bully who made your life a misery; the teacher who kept telling you that you were useless; or, the parent who kept criticising you for being 'lazy'.

In fact the 'PC' is the voice and echo of every negative experience you've ever had. And it doesn't stop there. It even invents voices of people who you *thought* were criticising you. It relives every experience you've ever had, X-raying it until it finds something it can criticise you about.

It ignores anything you may have done and focuses only on the negative. And indeed you help it along. You listen to it. You belittle any achievement that you may have had. You use excuses like 'Well, if I could pass the exam then anybody could have passed it' or 'If I got the job, there mustn't have been too many people applying for it' or 'they must have being desperate to take me'.

However this dismissive attitude towards your achievements is the direct opposite to how you view your mistakes. Oh no, the pathological critic doesn't dismiss those. All the mistakes you've ever made are kept in a safe place to be rehashed and used as another piece of evidence as to how big a failure you are.

The pathological critic is the *invalidating environment* running riot, unchecked in your head. It is firing 'evidence' so fast at you that you haven't a hope in switching it off without professional help.

Furthermore, as we saw in the last chapter, the pathological critic is always vague. So much so that even if you recognised that it's the PC that's criticising you, you could do very little about it.

By being vague, you can't focus on a target to fight against. For example, let's say that today you are punishing yourself because you didn't achieve a certain task or something like that. If you manage to focus on this particular incident, you may manage to convince yourself that getting one person's disapproval *doesn't* make you bad. Your PC however won't let you get that far.

As soon as there is a sign that you might get off the hook, the PC moves the goalposts and fires some other piece of evidence at you. 'Ah yeah, but what about that other task,' it says, and off you go again.

For every piece of evidence you manage to challenge, it has twenty more pieces ready to throw at you. And it's impossible to silence the critic's voice. Sometimes I will find that people have become so punch drunk that they have lost any willingness to try to do anything about it.

You see. In order to be depressed you have to accept that you're a failure. If you are willing to accept that this is not true then you will go back to the anxiety phase, i.e. afraid to go out and risk failing again. And for some, this is putting them into a world that is even more painful. For them it's easier to stay in the hole than climb out and be knocked in again.

Because the PC voices are coming from your emotional mind, they *feel* like they are correct. The reality though, is that *it is your thinking that's wrong, not you.*

Working with a therapist, hopefully they will help you to realise this. Realising that it's your thinking that is wrong and not you is the first step towards recovery. Learning to stop accepting everything your PC is telling you is the next.

Slowly, with the therapist's help you start looking much more carefully at what it is you are saying to yourself. Looking at each piece of evidence you examine as to whether it is accurate or not.

As you look at each piece and dispute it, you will start realising that the same pattern is happening over and over again. You start to realise that what you've accepted as truth for years is actually complete bullshit.

And like a snowball rolling downhill, this realisation gets greater and greater. Recovery gets easier and easier. In fact it gets a *lot* easier. Your logical and emotional minds gradually come into sync with each other until eventually you start reading life with your *wise* mind.

That is, you will realise, 'I *have* a problem rather than I *am* a problem.'

Or as Deirdre in Chapter 9 said: 'When little things get into my head, they remain . . . little things. For some reason, they don't go nuclear and take over my thinking.

'I still get anxious like everybody else. If I'm running late for a meeting I still freak out a bit, but freaking out a bit is as bad as it gets.'

The Solution

Once you have learned to identify the pathological critic you are now ready to go onto the next step. You see, learning that it is your thinking that is wrong helps you identify the problem. Learning *how* to fix it is what solves it.

Challenging your unhealthy/irrational beliefs is all very well and good, but what do you replace them with? To answer this, look at what you are trying to achieve by rating or measuring yourself.

Imagine you manage to achieve all your demands and are on top of the ladder. What's in it for you? What do you get if you have all this high self-esteem? Think about it. If you have high self-esteem you are temporally winning at your rating game.

So how will you feel? I suspect that you will feel on top of the world because you believe that 'I'm all right Jack'. You believe that you are all right because you've succeeded at all your measurements of achievement.

Now imagine you managed to learn that you could be OK regardless of whether you succeeded or not. Then you could feel on top of the world and that you're 'OK Jack' a whole lot more. Not only that, but you could get that 'on top of the world' feeling without having to do anything. A bit like winning the lotto without ever having to buy a ticket.

The solution of course is what we looked at in the last chapter. It is our old friend the Raggy Doll Club. And believe me, becoming a member of the Raggy Doll Club is the *only* solution.

In becoming a member you are showing willingness to accept yourself exactly as you are, that you can't be measured either by yourself or anybody else and that like everybody else, you make mistakes.

If you can just accept that you're no more mad/bad/sad than the rest of us you will start to achieve a sense of peace and serenity in your life that you never believed possible. Incidentally, you will also understand what it is like to be the most attractive person in the room.

In finishing this chapter I have to thank Cora. Cora was a graphic designer who had suffered from depression all her life. She had being attending a self-help group that I was working with in developing a model of CBT that could be incorporated into the group.

Cora really grasped the concept of the Raggy Doll Club and one day presented me with a drawing that she thought would be cool as a logo for the club. The logo was in the shape of a *No Entry* road sign with an = sign in it.

The meaning was clear. *No Entry* or in other words, there's no = sign in life. So why not give it a try.

Chapter 13

Habit 5: Abnormalising the Normal

In Chapter 3, I quoted a wise philosopher as saying that: 'None of us live in reality, we live in what we perceive our reality to be.'

You probably perceived it to be one of those clever quotations that you see from time to time that look good but don't really make sense to you and so ignored it.

Now it's time to start thinking about the statement a lot more as, in understanding how accurate it is, you will have an insight into why people can find it so hard to practise good mental health.

To illustrate what I mean, I'd like you to meet Andrea.

Andrea's Story

Andrea was a lady who came to see me about eleven years ago. She had been experiencing recurring bouts of depression over many years. Nothing she ever did could stop the depression from recurring.

She had visited numerous psychiatrists and therapists who helped her cope with the depression, but even though they gave her helpful advice as to what she should do for her mental health, poor Andrea could never manage it.

When she contacted me, she had just been discharged from hospital. At our first meeting Andrea gave me a brief overview of her history and then we both looked into how I might be able to help her. As Andrea was currently feeling OK when we met, I suggested that maybe this was a good opportunity to look at possible reasons as to why her depression kept being triggered.

We looked at what preceded all her previous bouts. This was a lot harder than you might think since I wanted Andrea to start looking at her problem from a very different perspective. Andrea said that the first thing she would notice was the anxiety.

This would begin for no apparent reason, but once it did, she would always find herself on a slippery slope downwards.

'I just can't stop it,' she said. 'No matter what I do I just can't seem to stop the spiral. I start off feeling anxious and then no matter what I do it's "Goodnight Julia" and off I go again.'

As this sounded suspiciously like the ego anxiety/ depression pathway that we looked at in the last chapter, I suggested that we look at the anxiety first and see where we went from there.

On asking for an example of when she felt anxious though, we ran into a problem. Because while Andrea thought and thought, she couldn't think of anything that she might be getting anxious about.

Now when this happens it's usually that the person has actually thought of what they were getting anxious about, but they don't realise it and dismiss the trigger as irrelevant. They don't recognise the connection between a seemingly innocuous trigger and their feeling.

I explained this to Andrea, but no matter how many

analogies I used, she still couldn't see anything that could be triggering her feeling. So we became like TV detectives, trying to find the culprit that was triggering Andrea's problem. Investigating more and more closely I asked her to recount when she first started the last anxious/depressed cycle.

The Traffic Jam

Andrea recounted how she first started feeling bad one Monday morning when she was travelling to work. I asked her how she travelled into work and she told me that she travelled on the M1 from Drogheda to Ballyfermot every day by car.

She said that she was stopped in traffic when she started to feel down. Delving even further I asked her to describe that scene more. Andrea said the she had just passed Junction 6 on the M1.

There had been a road traffic accident on the M50 and the resultant traffic was all the way back to Balbriggan. That's a 25 km traffic jam, by the way.

Andrea stated that it was a dark, rainy Monday morning in February. Nobody was going anywhere. It was then that she first noticed the feeling and realised that she was becoming unwell.

When training therapists, I try to teach them how to keep their mind working like a car that refuses to leave first gear. It may seem slow but you can see so much more of what's going on around you when you do. And the main advantage of this is that when a client says something that could be interpreted in two ways, you get confused immediately.

This results in the therapist looking for clarification, which can open whole new worlds of understanding. So it's like looking at each tree individually rather than the whole forest.

The confusion I was experiencing was that I couldn't quite see where she was getting her assumption that she was becoming unwell. What was she basing this on? Was it the traffic jam or how she was feeling at the time? What was happening that was leading her to conclude that she was becoming unwell?

I explained this to Andrea and asked her to think about what went through her mind *immediately before* she said to herself that she was becoming unwell. Andrea thought about this for a while.

She said that she just noticed herself feeling crap and it was this crap feeling that triggered her believing that she was getting unwell again.

'Mmmm,' I murmured. So because Andrea was feeling crap she had asserted to herself that she was becoming unwell. Andrea agreed with this. She also volunteered that by the end of that day, another bout of depression had started that lasted nearly two months.

I must admit, that while she was telling me about the events of that morning, I could identify with how she was feeling at the time. You see, I was travelling on the M1 that morning too and was stuck in the same traffic jam.

Where I was getting lost, however, was in the 'unwell' part. As I was stuck in the traffic jam I was feeling just as crap as she was. In fact I reckon most of the people stuck in the jam were feeling the same way.

Let's face it. It's a cold, wet, dark, wintry Monday morning. How do you expect to feel? Even one of the presenters on the radio was moaning about how wet he got on his way into work and how miserable he was feeling. And he wasn't stuck in our traffic jam.

So where was the 'unwell' bit coming in? Why, when she was feeling crappy like lots of people that morning, was Andrea concluding that she was unwell?

I put this to Andrea. I asked her to look at what she had just said. Where was her evidence that she was becoming unwell? And not for the first time, I was looked at as if I had suggested that the world was flat, but that's OK. I'm used to that.

However, getting looked at like that can mean a lot more. Andrea's assertion that she was becoming unwell had been stopped in its tracks. Probably for the first time, something that Andrea had always accepted categorically as fact was being challenged.

Like a lot of people, Andrea had always just accepted, without ever questioning, something her emotional mind was telling her.

'But I felt depressed sitting there,' she said. 'That's what always happens, I feel depressed and when I do, it all starts from there. I can't stop the slide and eventually end up in hospital.'

I then suggested that we inspect the scene even more closely and discover what exactly had happened at the time. Andrea recounted that whilst she was in the traffic jam, she felt a sense of something but she couldn't quite put a name on it – a kind of 'crappy' feeling.

'What kind of "crappy" feeling?' I asked.

'Kind of like a mixture of anxiety and depression,' she answered.

'So you were feeling the "Monday morning blues" then.' I said.

'Yes,' Andrea replied.

'So where did you pick it up that that was a sign of depression?' I challenged.

For the second time in as many minutes I got that look again.

'Well, if that's not a sign of depression, what is?' Andrea challenged back.

'I agree,' I said. 'Feeling down for a period of time is a symptom of depression. However you said that the feeling just came over you. Feeling the 'Monday morning blues' is not a sign of depression.

'Depression is when the "Monday morning blues" lasts for a few months. Not only that, but in order to be able to diagnose clinical depression, you must have more than just one symptom'.

To illustrate my point I reached over to my bookcase and took down my dog-eared copy of *The Diagnostic and Statistical Manual, Version 4.*

The Diagnostic and Statistical Manual (DSM) is one of those 'riveting reads' that health professionals use to help diagnose illnesses. Using categories, subcategories and plenty of 'section 1;1 sub section 2' language, the DSM 4 lists every mental illness known to man, categorises every symptom in every illness and lists them off.

It's about as interesting a read as a phone directory, but it does have its uses. Looking up Depression, I got Andrea to look at which symptoms she had at that particular moment on the motorway.

And do you know what? The only symptom she had at that time was the 'Monday morning blues'. However, by believing that she was becoming depressed due to this Monday morning feeling, Andrea was creating a much bigger problem for herself than just feeling crappy on a wet Monday.

What do I mean? Well let's do a chaining sequence on what happened:

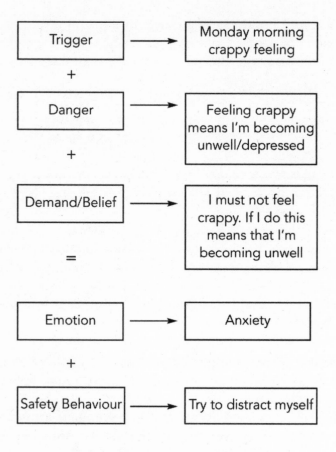

Fig. 18: Andrea's Anxiety Chain

And as we saw in the last chapter, this kicked off the anxiety phase of the ego anxiety/depressed pathway.

The Cycle

Of course the more she demanded not to feel down, the more down she felt. Therefore, she got more and more anxious until she eventually entered the depressed part of the cycle.

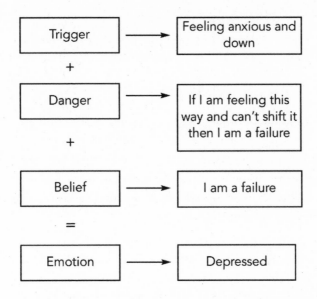

Fig. 19: Andrea's Depression Pathway

And so Andrea faced her next bout of Depression. Quite simply, Andrea had become 'anxious and depressed about being anxious and depressed'.

In psychotherapy we call this the *secondary problem*. A secondary problem is where the person attaches an interpretation/evaluation to the primary problem.

In Andrea's case, she had become 'depressed about being depressed'. However you don't have to have a history like Andrea's to find this kind of secondary problem.

Stephen, who we last met in Chapter 9, was doing something similar. Stephen was the student who was very anxious about going to college. As we saw, he was getting anxious about being anxious.

When teaching psychotherapists I try to make them understand that if the person is not responding to the therapy, this may be for two reasons:

1. That the client is not practising to the best of their ability what they are learning in therapy. (This is nearly always *not* the case.)

2. The client is trying to solve the wrong problem. (Most of the time, if the person is not responding to the therapy, this is the reason.)

In Stephen's case this is what he was doing. He was trying not to be anxious. However he didn't realise that what was preventing him from overcoming the anxiety was that he had two distinct anxieties going on:

1. He was anxious about going to college. This was accounting for about 30 percent of his problem.

2. Because he firmly believed that to get anxious was abnormal he was getting anxious about being anxious and this was accounting for 60 percent of his problem.

Fixing problem 1 is usually fairly straightforward, but if the person tries to cure their anxiety without first challenging problem 2, then they will end up doing the right thing for the wrong reason.

Everybody wants to soothe their anxiety and this is fine. However if you have major problems shifting it, then like Andrea and Stephen you may be making the same mistake.

When we reviewed Stephen's progress as therapy went on, we found the actual problem. By believing that to get anxious was a sign of abnormality, he was inadvertently demanding that he didn't get anxious.

He believed that if he could only overcome his anxiety he would in some way be normal. The mistake he was making though, was that he believed that he was abnormal if he felt any anxiety at all.

When we looked at what he was basing this on we found an entire ideology about what he thought a 'normal' person was that was completely at odds with reality. Many people do this.

They mistake feelings with illness. Harry Barry describes it very well. Depression and anxiety are what are commonly referred to as mood disorders. Without getting too technical, you can describe the difference as, 'Feelings are to weather as mood is to climate'

Put plainly, you can have crappy weather but you can't describe the climate unless you look at the weather over a period of time. In mental health terms, depression with a small 'd' is a crappy feeling that we all feel. Depression with a capital 'D' is when that crappy feeling lasts for a few months, combines with other symptoms and results in a change in the actual chemistry and structure of the brain.

Critical Incident Stress Debriefing

However, as we shall now see, the habit of constantly theorising about what 'normal' is crops up in a myriad of places. Some years ago, an approach to helping people overcome traumatic events was developed called *Critical Incident Stress Debriefing*, or CISD for short.

What CISD tried to do was provide a framework whereby people who had experienced bank robberies, bombings and all kinds of disasters could understand how they were feeling about what had happened and how they were subsequently affected by it.

When we would do a 'debriefing' session with a group we would use a specific formula where we would get the group to look at the chain of events that occurred during the incident, what thoughts went through their minds as the incident unfolded and finally what feelings they experienced both during and after the event.

However, in debriefing groups we would notice that whilst most of the group would find the process useful, one or maybe two would need more support than a CISD group could provide.

The curious thing about this group of people was that when I would speak to them after, I found that what they were saying to themselves about what they were feeling bothered them more than the actual event.

Elena's Story

Elena was a European girl who contacted me after she had been involved in a terrorist incident whilst on holiday. A bomb had exploded in the resort she was staying at. She was now experiencing all the hallmarks of *Post Traumatic Stress Disorder*.

Poor Elena would find herself getting panicky if she tried to sit in a café or anywhere where a crowd might be. She would try to relax but would find herself getting more and more anxious watching everybody in the café and where their bags were.

She had tried various therapies which she found didn't help the problem. When she arrived with me I did my usual and got my brain into first gear. What I noticed about her story wasn't that she was upset about the actual bombing.

What was upsetting Elena more was what she was saying about the way she was feeling. When I asked her how she felt about 'being anxious' she dropped the hand grenade right into my lap.

Looking me straight in the eye, Elena very simply said that she couldn't understand why she was feeling anxious. When I asked her to elaborate she stated that she could understand that it would be normal to be anxious if she had been in the vicinity of the bomb, but that when it had gone off, Elena was 20km away. She said that it wasn't reasonable to have PTSD as she was so far away from the bomb when it went off.

Of course, the only reasonable response I could make was to ask her how close to the bomb someone had to be in order to have a 'valid' PTSD. You see, Elena was not only anxious about the possibility of another bomb going off, she had attached a whole new relevance to the fact that she was getting anxious.

Like Andrea and Stephen above, Elena was getting *anxious about being anxious*. Or to put it another way, she was *abnormalising* her anxiety.

In order to help Elena overcome her PTSD, I first had to get her to accept that there was no definition as to what a 'normal' response was. Once she was able to accept this, overcoming her anxiety was made a whole lot easier.

Abnormalising the Normal

My experience has taught me that when people are finding it impossible to overcome their problem, it's usually because they are abnormalising their reaction. That is why, when we would run a CISD group, we would print the following statement on the literature: 'It was the situation that was abnormal, not you or your reactions.'

You see, those who experienced difficulties overcoming traumatic events were those who were abnormalising their reactions. The people who were able to accept that their feelings were normal and adopted the attitude of 'After what I've been through, what other way would you expect me to feel?' usually had a much easier recovery than those who were invalidating the way they were feeling and their reactions.

Look back to the chapter on 'Invalidating Environments'

and read it again. This is what is happening in people's minds that are falling into the habit of abnormalising the normal.

When we fall into this bad habit we start to change the way we view the world around us. We develop a vague idea of what way we *should* be and what way we *shouldn't* be.

We then build up a type of 'photo fit' image of what we think a 'normal' person is. We then compare ourselves to this photo fit image and when we don't measure up, we view ourselves as abnormal.

What people don't realise, or at least don't realise until they're sitting with me, is that it's their photo fit image that is abnormal, not them.

Trust me on this one. People have the most outlandish ideas about what they think 'normal' is which are completely out of touch with reality. I hope that in reading what I've written throughout this book you can discover some of your own beliefs about what 'normal' is.

Furthermore, secondary problems like the habit of forcing oneself to be 'normal' are usually what's behind people experiencing extreme difficulty in overcoming what are usually common or garden neurotic problems.

And if you don't believe me, then let's look at where the habit presents in all its glory. Where it is so common that I see it every day, everywhere I go. It is in people who believe that they must suffer in silence, potentially for years, for fear of what it will say about them, if people know they are suffering. It is nowhere more prominent than in what is commonly referred to as *Postnatal Depression*.

Postnatal Depression

We first met Louise at the start of Chapter 1. She was the woman who was sitting in the coffee shop with the baby feeling miserable. After struggling for so many months Louise had finally decided to bite the bullet and seek help.

Of course, 'biting the bullet' and deciding to seek help was the hard part. Many people think (or at least those that aren't depressed) that if you are feeling bad, then getting help is a fairly straightforward step in resolving the problem.

Not so. You see, finally deciding to seek help and then doing it can be the hardest part of recovery. Why? Give it some thought. Actually taking the step towards help is the easy part. Coping with what you say to yourself about the fact that you're taking this step is the hard part.

In Louise's head, like in many other people's heads, seeking help was like accepting that she really *was* a failure. If she wasn't a failure then why would she have to accept help? After all, you don't end up seeing a shrink like me because you're singing too loudly in the church choir, do you?

When I interviewed Louise for this book she told me that she had never felt as low as she did the day that she came to see me. She said that before she met me, coming to see me meant that she had now to accept every negative thing that she had being saying about herself. However, as Louise found out, and as I hope you will find out, *out of breakdowns come breakthroughs*.

One of the first things you should realise is that seeking help is no more significant than consulting your GP for a chest infection that just won't shift. However, since the person often has to get over their irrational thinking about coming to see me *without* help, it can be a very difficult step for them to take.

The reality is that once people meet me and realise that I'm no different to them, they usually relax.

So having got the formalities over and Louise realising that I didn't bite, we got to the 'meat and two vegetables' of why she was with me. Louise described her experience of motherhood and how difficult she was finding it.

All her life she had regarded herself as a very competent person, but she just couldn't manage to 'get it right' with the baby.

Puzzled, I asked her to tell me what she wasn't 'getting right'.

'Everything,' she replied.

'Well could you give me an example of something that you're not getting right?' I specified.

Louise sat for a few moments. She said that she couldn't really identify one thing, but she just had this overwhelming feeling that she couldn't cope like normal mums even though she was working so hard at it.

'And could you tell me how a "normal" mum copes?' I asked.

Louise told me afterwards that at this point, she suddenly regretted coming to see me. She thought to herself that she should have gone to see a female therapist. The fact that I had asked such a nonsensical question 'showed' that I must know little or nothing about being a mother.

And she's not the only one who has thought that when they look at me with my best deadpan expression, asking such a question. And deadpan is the operative word in how I handle situations like this when I'm asking mums to describe what they think a 'normal' mother is like.

You see, by giving the deadpan look, I'm inviting mums to 'teach' me all about what being a mother *should* be like. The fun and games begin when they try to describe their theory on this. Because of all the irrational theories that people believe and use to guide their lives, the concept of what people believe a 'normal' mum should be like is easily the most irrational.

Louise described that she saw other mums coping without feeling as bad as she did.

'And how do you know how they are feeling?' I challenged. 'How can you "know" by looking at them what they are feeling? Are they transparent?'

I then asked her to describe to me what she thought a 'proper' mother was like. Louise, like a lot of mums in her position, had a vague idea that proper mothers didn't get depressed or anxious.

Proper mothers, in her eyes didn't get stressed out like she did and didn't 'freak out' with anxiety when their baby wouldn't take their feed. At this point I asked Louise if I could interrupt her just to clarify something.

You see, having worked in this job for years and having watched my wife trying to cope with our two boys, I was lost as to where Louise was getting her concept of the 'proper' mother.

I asked her did she know of any mother who had all these wonderful attributes, because I sure as blazes would love to meet them. Louise said that she didn't know them personally, but that she had always accepted that the other women she saw with babies were like that.

She described the woman with blonde hair that she used to see with her baby around town. Between sessions I asked Louise to think about what she believed other mothers who were 'proper' were like and to give me some evidence of someone who fit that bill.

At the next session we looked at the results of her 'investigation'. Louise said that she hadn't been able to think of anyone. I then suggested to her that maybe, just maybe, what was at fault was her concept of what she thought a 'normal' mum was, not her.

If Louise was willing to accept this, or rather if I could even get her to be willing to be willing to accept this, I could then proceed to step two. You see, in step two, I was going to illustrate for Louise what a 'normal' mum was *really* like.

The Real Mother Experience

I started by explaining that when you have a baby it is perfectly normal to get stressed out. In the hospital, you're handed this baby and find out very suddenly that from now on, no matter what happens, the buck will now stop with you.

During those first few years, expect to be stressed out. On top of that, expect to be showing all the signs and symptoms of severe sleep deprivation. Sleep deprivation is a very effective method of torture used by intelligence organisations to create an emotional state in victims where depression, anxiety, confusion and despair can be easily triggered.

And if that's not enough, your whole world has just been turned upside down. Once the baby arrives you go from coffee with the girls and baby showers to nappies, faeces and vomit. Then there's the effect of crying.

Look around you at a group of young children who are laughing and making noise when they are watching a stage magician. Look at the adults, most of them will be relaxed and smiling at all the squeals of delight from the kids.

Now look at what happens in a restaurant when a child starts to cry. All the adults start to feel uncomfortable. If the crying doesn't stop fairly soon, people start to leave.

I have a friend who used to say that his youngest son had a cry 'that would clear a restaurant'. Even though the decibel level is much less than the group of laughing kids, the crying has that special quality that's like a knife scraping across metal.

And that's precisely what Mother Nature has designed it for. To get a reaction from you so that you will do *anything* to stop it. Effective, isn't it? Now imagine having a child crying in your ear for extended periods of time. Combine it with the sleep deprivation and I'm sure you get the idea.

At this stage you're starting to get very stressed and

anxious. Experiencing this is bad enough. However the post-natal period is only the starter. For our main course we can add the guilt and the effect all of this has on your relation-ships with those around you.

Dr Mary Rogan is a well-known 'roll up your sleeves', down-to-earth GP and psychosexual therapist working in Galway. In trying to help mothers who come to see her for help she uses a wonderful quote that encapsulates the diffi-culties that mothers the world over can identify with: 'A mother's place is in the wrong.'

This speaks for itself. But for those of you who would like the scientific reasoning behind it then think about this.

The cognitive dynamic of guilt is when we demand of ourselves, 'I absolutely must know what to do and be able to do it'.

What this means is that as far as your children are con-cerned, no matter what happens with them, you will hold yourself totally responsible for everything about them. You must both come up with a solution and ensure that it's imple-mented.

And you will still run with your irrational demand that you *should*, when things that even experts have no solution for and are absolutely outside your control to solve, happen.

The demand is so intrinsic in you that it runs to the very fibre of your being. So no matter how successful you are and no matter what you achieve, you will still find something to feel guilty about.

On top of this your sexual libido is completely switched off. We believe that this is as a result of the secretion of a sub-stance called oxytocin that is released immediately after childbirth. Its effect is to cause your uterus to contract extremely strongly so as to clamp off the blood vessels that were supplying the baby.

Unfortunately, it also switches off your sexual drive.

Makes sense when you think about it. Mother Nature is ensuring that you won't feel the urge to get pregnant for some time. Alas it is in the misinterpretation of this that causes many problems with your spouse.

Did you know that 10 percent of fathers experience post-natal depression? Why? Try to look at it from *their* perspective. What they see is that you have gone from having that 'I want to have your baby' look to looking at them like they're a nappy disposal unit.

What they are misinterpreting is the fact that your need for them is greater *after* the birth than it was before. It's just different, that's all. Of course, for the dad, what he sees is that you're rejecting him.

This leaves him feeling very insecure in the relationship. And guess how he tries to get his security back? Yes, you've guessed it, by trying to have sex with you.

And of course with your libido in your boots, this is the last thing you need, so you refuse, which reinforces his sense of rejection. So he tries again. You refuse again. A vicious cycle begins that causes huge problems in your relationship. He feels more and more insecure and you feel more and more guilty.

You wouldn't believe how many times I've seen couples experience this problem. And all because both parties are misinterpreting the other. He is misinterpreting your actions and behaviour and, believe it or not, the woman is misinterpreting *his* behaviour.

Remember, his looking for sex is so that he will feel secure about your need for him. And to give him this sense of security and love *you don't have to have sex with him.*

What I teach women is to do the simple things that will give him this. Smile at him when he comes home. Give him a kiss goodbye when he goes out to work in the morning. Tell him frequently what you feel about him and how you need him. And would you believe, taking these simple actions can go a long way to reassuring him and calming tensions.

The Main Course

So now you've had the starter and the main course. Let's throw in a bit of dessert to complete our meal. Remember in Chapter 11, I described how because we are human we all have ego anxiety and that ego anxiety is the anxiety that is triggered when we don't measure up to whatever it is we rate ourselves on. Well mix this belief into what I've just described above.

If you believe that as a mum you are always in the wrong, then it's only a matter of time before you start to get ego anxious. The result of this is that you will start to try even *harder* to get everything 'right'.

Of course, the more you try to get it right, the more you will see yourself getting it wrong. Eventually, all you will see is the *wrong*. And as most women will see this as 'I'm a failure', you will get depressed from time to time or as Dr Harry Barry calls it, feel 'depression with a small "d"'.

Coping With the Baby

So, if this is the normal experience after you have a baby, how are you supposed to cope with it? Well, actually you don't. You don't 'learn' to cope with it. What you do is 'white knuckle' it and eventually the kids grow up. And trust me, it does get easier.

The experience I've just described is very normal. The experts call this postnatal 'distress' or you could call it postnatal depression with a small 'd'.

But how does this Postnatal pistress become Postnatal

Depression with a capital 'D'? To illustrate how this happens, let's go back to Louise and do a simple chaining sequence on what she was saying to herself about the way she was feeling.

For Louise, as with all cases of postnatal depression that I see, the problem isn't the baby or even the way she is feeling. The problem is always about what the mum is saying to herself about the way she is feeling.

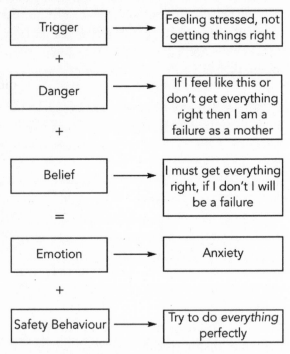

Fig. 20: Louise's Anxiety Chain

You see, Louise firmly believed that it was abnormal to be feeling stressed out, and as such created a chain reaction in her thinking about this.

Of course, Louise wasn't doing everything perfectly in order to *be* perfect. She believed that she must make everything perfect in order to be just OK. And of course, the more perfect she tried to be, the more imperfect she realised she was, until all she could see was what she was getting wrong.

And therein lay the problem. For Louise was making the same cognitive error as Elena and Andrea above. Instead of having one problem, Louise had two.

Her first problem was that she was finding coping with a baby very stressful. This was difficult enough. But for Louise, her second problem was what was making her first problem virtually impossible to deal with.

You see, whenever Louise experienced any difficulty, instead of being able to come up with coping strategies, she spent all her energies on scolding herself for experiencing the difficulty in the first place.

And it's not only Louise who experiences this. I see it every day, everywhere I go. Mums struggling, trying to prevent anybody seeing how much they are suffering for fear of what they perceive people will think if they find out.

I started this book by telling Louise's story and I'm finishing with her story. I would have loved to have been able to end this book by saying that I performed some slick manoeuvre that caused her to realise at an emotional level what I was trying to teach her, but I can't.

Louise's 'cure' came from a source that neither of us could have foreseen at the time. The story I outlined at the start of the book occurred after the session that I described above. Louise had only attended my practice a few times and whilst at some level she had understood what I was talking about, in her head she didn't really believe it.

So let's conclude this book by finishing the story of what happened when she went back to the coffee shop to get the baby's bottle heated.

The Woman In the Coffee Shop

Do you recall the blonde woman in Louise's story with whom she used to compare herself? For Louise, this woman represented everything that Louise wasn't. She seemed in control, confident and competent.

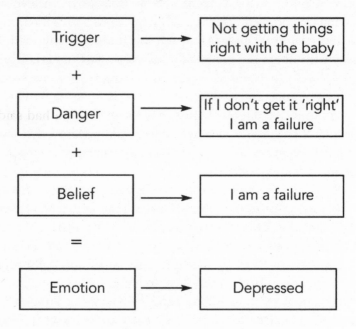

Fig. 21: Louise's Depression Pathway

As Louise went into the café again, she was horrified to see that the blonde woman was still sitting there. Louise was mortified that she was now going to have to let her see that she had forgotten to get the bottle heated before she had left the last time.

As she waited at the counter, she noticed out of the corner of her eye that the woman was coming over to her. Louise was horrified. 'Oh god,' she thought. 'She's going to ask me do I need some help'.

266

To Louise this was her worst case scenario. 'I'm so bad, everybody can see,' she thought. Cringing and wishing the ground would open up and swallow her, she waited for the blonde woman to reach her.

The woman smiled as she reached Louise. 'Hi,' she said. 'I'm Aisling. I'm so glad you came back because I've so wanted to speak to you for so long but didn't have the nerve to approach you. When I saw you walk back in I decided to go for it so here I am. Would you like to share a cup of coffee?'

Louise felt confused. She felt trapped that she couldn't say no, but also, neither could she grasp what Aisling had said. Both of them sat down at the table. Aisling commented that she was so glad to have approached Louise as she really needed to make friends with someone who was in the same boat.

'Jeez,' she said. 'If anybody else gets all sentimental with me, I'll throttle them. I can't believe that it's so hard.

'Nobody ever warned me that it was going to be like this. It's just so wonderful to have someone who's going through it as well to be able to chat to'.

Aisling chatted on and on. Louise found her so easy to listen to. They talked about their babies, husbands, milk formulas and everything that they both had in common. Louise could have stayed there for hours. However, as the baby was soon due a feed, Louise had to head home.

As she walked along the street, she felt a new lightness about herself that she hadn't experienced before. Louise thought about Aisling and how funny she made the entire baby thing sound. The more Louise thought about it the more she found herself giggling at things Aisling had said. Aisling might be finding motherhood as rough as Louise, however she was able to see the 'gallows humour' about it. Why was that?

Suddenly it struck her. Aisling might be finding it as tough, but the reason she was able to see the lighter side was because she was able to recognise that to be feeling crap was *normal*. Louise was stunned. Out of the blue she remembered that this was what I had been trying to say to her.

Feeling crap was normal. It didn't mean that she was a crap mother if she was finding it difficult. Neither did it mean that in order to be just OK she had to get everything 100 percent right.

Louise realised that even though she wasn't doing it the way she felt she should, *she didn't have to*. As long as she managed to get through tonight without anything too serious happening then she would be fine.

She would survive. The baby would eventually leave this phase and Louise knew that it would get easier. As she walked along the road Louise thought about this realisation. Since the baby had arrived she had been terrified of the little bundle that was now hers.

And with the terror came the shame that she would never be like what she thought proper mothers were like. Now she had met another mum who openly admitted that she was feeling the same as Louise.

However Aisling felt no shame whatsoever. In fact, even with finding it so difficult she was able to keep it all in perspective. She smiled at a saying she once heard, that the knack of keeping things in perspective with your kids is to, 'Keep them breathing and out of jail, everything else is a bonus'.

And Louise just knew that this was as hard as it would get but so what? 'I've managed so far,' she thought.

With that she noticed a new freedom and a new happiness come over her. 'Maybe I'm not doing too badly after all,' she thought. 'My baby is healthy. Maybe he does cry a lot but so what. It's only a phase.

'He'll grow out of it. I only have to cope until bedtime tonight. Tomorrow will probably be just as bad, but I haven't ended up in a home for the bewildered yet. If I can just get a few hours' sleep I'll be able to cope.'

Picking up her stride she started to look forward to the evening. 'Sod it,' she thought. 'I couldn't be bothered cooking tonight. We eat healthily all the time. Let's just order a pizza and cuddle up for the evening.'

It was then that Louise realised that she had become a member of the Raggy Doll Club.

Chapter 14

Hasten Slowly, Get Well Gently

So now that it's time to wrap up I would like to tell you a story about an encounter I had some time ago whilst I was writing this book.

I am very fortunate to be married to a very beautiful Chinese woman and, as such, spend a lot of time in her home city in northeast China. About two years ago a number of health professionals working in mental health approached my wife and asked if I would run a workshop where we could compare western and eastern approaches to overcoming depression and anxiety.

I must admit I was fascinated to find how they approach mental health issues in China so, facilitated by my lovely wife who is bilingual, we all met up during one of my visits there.

When we started talking, the first thing that amazed both them and me was how similar our experiences were. Once we got beneath the superficial cultural differences that separate us we found that the stresses that people encounter in China were exactly the same that people encounter here in Ireland.

Not only that but, when people presented looking for help, they presented the same way in China as they did in Ireland. When people sought help, the stories and problems the Chinese were hearing were no different to the stories and problems that I hear every day.

Within a very short time I found that I was as comfortable sitting at this multi-disciplinary meeting as I would be at any similar meeting in Ireland. We all spoke a common language of mental health that made understanding each other very easy.

When we got down to the nitty gritty of how we try to help people overcome their difficulties, lo and behold we also found that we all had very similar approaches in trying to help people.

This was not because China was adopting western ideals. No, Chinese attitudes to good mental health and how to practise it had evolved independently.

As the workshop progressed I decided to try to introduce the idea of the Raggy Doll Club to them and see what they thought of it. I braced myself for the backlash when I did this as when I introduce the concept of unconditional self and other acceptance to groups in the west, people can be very challenging as to what they think they have heard.

Not so with the Chinese group. As I spoke about the Raggy Doll Club and presented it as one of the essential building blocks in mental health, I felt as if I was pushing an open door. They didn't challenge me in any shape or form.

Did they understand me? Were they disagreeing with me and just being very Chinese in not challenging me? I must admit, I was a bit put out. I could handle being challenged or being asked to explain differently, but with this group they just sat there silently looking at me.

They said nothing, nada, zilch. Not a word. After a while I kicked for touch and suggested a coffee break. During it I gently asked one of the therapists if they had understood what I had being talking about.

'Of course,' she said. 'We have the same concept. You call it "unconditional self acceptance", we call it Confucianism.'

She then went on to explain that the ideas I had introduced as being at the heart of CBT thinking in the west had been described by Confucius thousands of years ago.

A few days later I met with some members of the group again. As a memento of the workshop they presented me with a beautiful vase. On it was a quotation written in Chinese from Confucius. It simply said:

Learn to be the fool occasionally.

What a lovely way of practising being a Raggy Doll!

And there we have it. As I said at the beginning of the book, what I've written is not the Gospel according to Enda Murphy. Rather it's what I've learned is the only way of being happy and having a contented, fulfilling life.

Remember, nobody has a patent on mental health or the best way of achieving it. If all the authors of mental health books and therapies are honest, they will admit that all they are doing is regurgitating and repackaging basic philosophies that have been around for thousands of years.

Very close to where I live there is an ancient passage grave called a barrow from about 4000 BC. What this says is that people have being living on my lane for thousands of years.

In the evenings as I sit with my wife and we talk about the kids and our plans for the future, I sometimes reflect that thousands of others over thousands of years have sat where I'm sitting having very similar conversations.

And I'm sure those same conversations have been about the same problems. Putting food on the table, trying to protect our families and of course what the neighbours might be thinking of us.

And if the problems are all similar then the solutions that the 'wise old owls' have come up with over the centuries are equally similar. Don't take my word for it, look around you.

Look at what all the different philosophies say is the best way to live.

If, like I did in China, you manage to get beneath the superficial differences between these philosophies then you will find that they are all basically saying the same thing. The philosophies are very simple and straightforward. It is us who complicate them and try to change them to suit our thinking and attitude.

When I was asked to write a book on my experience I said I could do it on the back of an envelope. Don't believe me? Well look at this.

The Five Habits of Unhappy People

1. The Panic Attack Cycle: Getting anxious about being anxious and believing that the actual physical symptoms of anxiety can be dangerous to you.

2. Trying to be in Control: Demanding that you must have 100 percent stability, certainty, security and order in your life 100 percent of the time. Remember, the skill of a happy life is in learning how to cope with the instability, uncertainty, insecurity and disorder of life without getting anxious.

3. The Social Anxiety Trap: Believing that you are whatever people think you are. By believing this, you are putting an = sign in who you are that is just not true. And the only cure I know for this habit is to become a member of the Raggy Doll Club.

4. The Depression Cycle: Where you put the = sign in how you rate yourself. Namely that you believe that you can be measured by this and that. Once again, the only cure is the Raggy Doll Club.

5. Abnormalising the Normal: Be very careful in what you believe to be normal. Saying that something is 'normal for me' is equally irrational, as you are saying to yourself that you should be allowed live by different rules to the rest of us.

Of course, describing and understanding the habits is only useful if it points you in the direction of finding a solution. Mental health is not rocket science. Understanding the dynamics of good mental health and knowing what to do to practise it should be no more complicated than understanding the dynamics of good physical health and knowing how to be healthy.

If you believe that you are one of those people who can't change, then ask yourself this: Was it that I couldn't change or that I didn't know *how* to change? In the vast majority of cases it's the latter.

Remember, no matter how you grew up, no matter what has happened to you, you *can* change the way you feel. If you don't believe me then look around you. People are changing every day.

Every day people are changing things in their lives. We change fashions. We change jobs. We even change relationships. Every day in every way we are changing to adapt to our changing lives.

So why not change according to some very simple rules that are easier to practise than you think. Don't think that you have to do it alone. People are practising changing all around you.

You'll find them in local clubs, fitness groups and educational classes. They are to be found in the vast number of self-help groups from Alcoholic Anonymous to Grow to Aware.

People everywhere are changing. It doesn't matter which philosophy or method you follow. Most of them should have very similar ideals. It's just the language they use in presenting their message that's different.

Find one that appeals to you and just give it a lash. As a wonderful poem by Max Ehrmann called 'Desiderata' says:

With all its sham, drudgery and broken dreams,
it is still a beautiful world.
Strive to be happy.

Flagging the Problem:
A New Approach to Mental Health

As Irish society undergoes rapid change and the pace of modern life seems ever faster, it is unsurprising that the issue of mental health has become more prominent and, thankfully somewhat more openly discussed – and the provision of treatment better and more widely available. *Flagging The Problem: A New Approach to Mental Health* is made up of five main sections – each section marked with a coloured flag that represents a particular mental state or area of concern: the Green Flag explains the normal mood system, the Red Flag deals with depression, the Yellow Flag addresses anxiety, the Purple Flag deals with addiction and the White Flag addresses the issue of suicide. There is a technical section, and extra appendices at the end of the book including information on self-help groups, and a list of commonly used medicines.

ISBN: 9781905483976 | €14.99
Available from all good bookshops and from libertiespress.com
Trade Orders to Gill and Macmillan:
Telephone: +353 (1) 500 9534 | E-mail: sales@gillmacmillan.ie

Flagging the Therapy: Pathways Out of Depression and Anxiety

From the best-selling 'Flagging' series, Flagging the Therapy examines the numerous medical, psychological and complimentary therapies that can all help in negotiating a pathway out of depression and anxiety.

'Dr Barry's first book was truly unique. In *Flagging the Therapy* he develops his highly accessible approach to mental health with a particular emphasis on how different treatments for depression, anxiety and other psychological problems work. Another superb contribution from one of Ireland's most insightful doctors.'

Dr Muiris Houston, *medical correspondent, Irish Time*

ISBN: 9781907593147 | €16.99
Available from all good bookshops and from libertiespress.com
Trade Orders to Gill and Macmillan:
Telephone: +353 (1) 500 9534 | E-mail: sales@gillmacmillan.ie

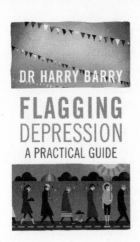

Flagging Stress: Toxic Stress and How to Avoid It

Flagging Stress: Toxic Stress and How to Avoid It is a comprehensive guide to recognising the symptoms of stress and learning to cope with it in our everyday lives.

Stress comes from multiple of sources, including pressures at work, relationship difficulties and illness. Most people can usually take what life throws at them, but when stress builds up, it can overwhelm an individual and lead to potentially serious health problems like depression, heart disease, obesity and chronic pain. With the right tools, we can learn how to manage it. Taking a new, fresh approach, *Flagging Stress* is just such a tool. Identifying the different kinds of stress – and in particular the dangers of 'toxic' stress, Dr Barry shows us how to identify where our stress is coming from and how we can effectively confront, manage and reduce it in our lives.

ISBN: 9781905483310 | €12.99
Available from all good bookshops and from libertiespress.com
Trade Orders to Gill and Macmillan:
Telephone: +353 (1) 500 9534 | E-mail: sales@gillmacmillan.ie

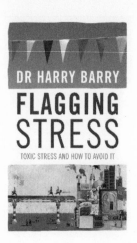

Flagging Depression:
A Practical Guide

The fourth instalment of Dr Harry Barry's best-selling 'Flagging' series, *Flagging Depression* not only reaches out to those dealing with depression, but also their friends and family, offering vital assistance. With a foreword by Paul Kelly of Console, *Flagging Depression* lays out a practical four step approach with particular emphasis on how to feel better, get better and stay well.

ISBN: 9781907593413 | €13.99

Available from all good bookshops and from libertiespress.com

Trade Orders to Gill and Macmillan:

Telephone: +353 (1) 500 9534 | E-mail: sales@gillmacmillan.ie